The Bilingual Family

Second Edition

The Bilingual Family

A handbook for parents

Second Edition

Edith Harding-Esch and Philip Riley

CAMBRIDGE
UNIVERSITY PRESS

CAMBRIDGE UNIVERSITY PRESS
Cambridge, New York, Melbourne, Madrid, Cape Town, Singapore, São Paulo, Delhi

Cambridge University Press
The Edinburgh Building, Cambridge CB2 8RU, UK

www.cambridge.org
Information on this title: www.cambridge.org/9780521808620

First published 1986
Second edition 2003
4th printing 2007

Printed in the United Kingdom at the University Press, Cambridge

A catalogue record for this publication is available from the British Library

ISBN 978-0-521-80862-0 hardback
ISBN 978-0-521-00464-0 paperback

This book is dedicated to:

Philip and Emma; Emily, Finn and Katja; Carine and Lydia; Nicolas, Matthias and Jerôme; Roselyn and Etienne; Antoine and Amélie; Marianne and Erik; Anna and Jon; Ellen, John and Jenny; Patrick and Michael; Peter; Anne and Dominic; Dominique, Claire and Stéphanie; Billy, Lia and Alexis; Joanna; Helena and Philip; Lisa and Ian; Wided, Cihame and Sophian; Sebastian, José, Francisco, Trinidad and Manuel; Alvin; Eliot and Robin; David; and to their parents.

Contents

The authors

Edith Harding-Esch
Edith Harding-Esch, who is French, is Senior Research Fellow in Language Education at the University of Cambridge and a former member of the *Centre de Recherches et d'Applications Pédagogiques en Langues* (CRAPEL) at the University of Nancy. She was married to an English mathematician and they have two children, Emma and Philip. The family's language is French, English being kept for work and studies. Philip and Emma do not have children yet.

Philip Riley
Before settling in France, Philip Riley, who is English, taught in universities in Finland and Malta. He now works at the *Centre de Recherches et d'Applications Pédagogiques en Langues* (CRAPEL) at the University of Nancy, and has published extensively on linguistics and language teaching. He is married to a Swedish-speaking Finn and they have three children. While the children were young, they spoke English and Swedish at home and French at school. Emily, the eldest, has married a Frenchman and now has two children of her own, Robin and Eliot, who are learning English and French. Finn and Katja do not have children yet.

Preface

This is a handbook for all parents who might be considering bringing up their children as bilinguals. It is written for the English-speaking family living in Stuttgart, or Madrid or Strasbourg, the Spanish woman who has settled in Germany or the Danish family who live in North America. It is not about bilingual societies: we will not talk about the distribution of speakers of different languages in countries such as Finland or Wales. The linguistic problems of immigrant groups are not discussed either: they involve social and political issues that go well beyond the scope of this book.

Although a majority of our examples concern European families, what we have to say will also be relevant to parents in many other parts of the world. In the same way, although many, but not all, of our case studies refer to professional families, we believe that the book should be useful to the wider range of increasingly mobile families who are faced with the problem of educating their children in two or more languages. What we have aimed at here is to help, inform and reassure parents by making available to them the experiences of a number of other families. The term 'family' refers to the social unit formed by any parent(s) plus children.

We have no particular theoretical or psychological axe to grind: this is not a set of dogmatic, hard and fast rules, but rather a practical discussion of some of the basic issues that we hope will help parents in their own particular situation. The book starts with a brief presentation of the uses to which all children, bilingual or not, put language, as well as with the definition of a small number of terms that are useful to talk about language and language acquisition. The major part of the book, however, is devoted to:

i) A summary of the research which has been done on bilingualism and on the development of the bilingual child.

ii) A discussion of the factors which parents should take into consideration when deciding whether to bring up their children as bilinguals.

iii) A series of case studies of a wide variety of bilingual families, where readers will be able to see the different choices and decisions made by parents in different contexts.

iv) An alphabetical reference guide to a number of topics or notions likely to be useful to parents.

We would like to emphasise that, although we are both professional linguists, it is the direct, personal and daily experience of bilingualism in our own families which has motivated the book. Readers may not agree with all we have to say, or may find that it does not apply to their particular situation; indeed, it would be surprising if this were not sometimes the case. It would have been impossible to offer a comprehensive treatment of all possible cases; we simply tried to formulate what our first-hand experience over many years has taught us.

Our subject, bringing up bilingual children, is only one aspect of that vast and controversial problem of bringing up children. In any family, there is a wide range of factors influencing the relationships between the individual members (for example, social roles, health, age, religious and political views) which are not linguistic but which are crucial in defining the members' and the family's identities. We are no more competent to talk about these things than any other parents, and so we have tried not to allow our personal views to colour the discussion that follows. Bilingual children are children first and foremost and problems like pocket money or puberty are just as pressing for them as for anyone else. Dealing with only one aspect of a child's life is a risky enterprise, forced upon us by the complexity of the subject, but we are well aware of the importance of the overall context, of the *whole* child.

In the past fifteen years or so, there have been many developments in the field of bilingual studies, which is one of the main reasons for producing this second edition. In particular, there has been a great increase in research and there are now several established international journals regularly reporting on bilingual and multilingual development. Much work has been carried out on the societal aspects of bilingualism (Fishman, 1989), including major studies dealing with language death (Fishman, 1991; Crystal, 2000; Nettle and Romaine, 2000). There have also been numerous descriptive studies, especially in the fields of language contact, code-switching and language change (Milroy and Muysken, 1995; Jones and Esch, 2002), as well as theoretical studies in cultural variation in language use, anthropological linguistics (Duranti, 1997; Foley, 1997) and cognitive anthropology (Gumperz and Levinson, 1996) which have all contributed to lively debates on the relationship between thought and language and to a reassessment of the Sapir-Whorf hypothesis on linguistic relativity.

Bilingual education has also received a great deal of attention, both in the USA (Hornberger, 1990) and in Europe (Baker, 2001), where the work of the Council of Europe leading to the publication of the Common European Framework of Reference for Languages (Council of Europe, 2001) has gone hand-in-hand with the promotion of plurilingualism and pluriculturalism. The project has been given even greater impetus by the various events organised throughout Europe during the European Year of Languages 2001. This has been accompanied by the introduction of programmes teaching foreign languages to children in primary school in a number of countries. At the same time there has been a growing awareness of linguistic minorities, resulting in increased stress being placed on the importance of interculturality for individuals and on the realisation that language development and language use are closely related, both being grounded in a unique social and cultural context (Byram, 1997b; Roberts et al., 2001; Kramsch, 1998; DeLoache and Gottlieb, 2000).

However, it has to be admitted that there has been relatively little progress as regards educating one's own children bilingually, a topic which has been further complicated by radical changes in the family as a social unit over the period in question, so that there are now 'a greater variety of household forms in modern society in which the nuclear family is not the most prevalent' (Turner, 1999). We have tried to take these developments into account in this new edition. It is important to understand that, socially speaking, the undoubted increase in bilingual families reflects the fact that, to quote Turner again, there are more and more 'modified extended families in which there are important kinship networks between relatives who do not live with each other, and also a widespread dependence on non-kin relations for support'. None the less, the central function of the family, of whatever shape or size, is still that of providing affection, intimacy and general well-being, and this is why although we have carefully updated this edition, the overall contents and thrust are not vastly different from the first edition.

Before launching into a more detailed discussion of bilingualism, there is one general point we would like to make. It is one that tends to be forgotten, especially by professional linguists, psychologists and teachers when talking about this matter. It is that the vast majority of bilinguals themselves find their bilingualism both ordinary and fruitful. In the past, so much work on bilingualism has been carried out by monolingual scientists who regarded it with a mixture of admiration and fear, that the experience and opinions of bilingual individuals themselves were pushed into the background. If you interview bilinguals, as we have done, you will find that nearly all of them value and enjoy their bilingualism, finding in it a source of interest and enrichment. For children, in particular, it is quite literally fun and games.

We would be extremely pleased to hear from any parents or children who have comments to make about this book. We would also like to thank the many parents who have written to us over the years, sharing their experience of raising bilingual children. Wherever possible, we have tried to take their observations into account.

Finally, we would like to make the following two points:

i) Where an actual boy or girl is not being referred to, we have alternated the use of 'he' and 'she' between chapters rather than use the male or female pronoun throughout.

ii) When the two languages of a bilingual individual are mentioned, the first language is the one in which the individual is considered to be dominant. However, particularly with children, the stronger language may become the weaker in a very short time (see section 3.3) which explains why the same individual's languages may appear in a different order at different ages.

E.H.-E., P.R.
September 2002

I

A survey of the issues

....

CHAPTER ONE

Children and language

What do children use language for?

In this section, we will be looking at the various stages that all children go through when they start talking. However, it is important to remember that we cannot see what is actually going on inside a child's head, so that despite the intense scrutiny that has been made in recent years of the ways in which children acquire language, much of the mystery remains. This is one reason why we will concentrate on what children actually *do* with language, since that can be observed and studied by an outsider. A second reason is that it is of far greater relevance to their relationships with their parents than most technical studies, which tend to deal with such topics as the order in which certain fine points of grammar are acquired, or the connection between language and the physiology of the brain. For example, it is possible to analyse in great detail how a child gradually acquires the complex grammar of negation, but when Eliot (2 yrs 1 mth) says 'No Teletubbies!' his mother needs to know whether he wants her to change TV channels or not.

1.1   Building up relationships

– Morning.
– Morning.
– Bit nippy, isn't it?
– Yes. Really nippy.
– Oh well.
– Yes, well. See you.
– See you.

We spend much of our lives building up and maintaining social relationships by means of rituals of this kind. If we look at the actual content of such exchanges, at what is actually *said*, we find that they are almost totally bereft of meaning. But if we look at their functions, at what is *done*, we see that they are of very great importance: quite literally, they hold society together.

Try to imagine what would happen if next time you met your neighbour in the lift and he said: 'Hello', you did not answer. Not to return a greeting is to shun someone's society, almost to deny their existence, which is why we get so upset if it ever happens to us.

Moreover, in most circumstances, no other serious conversation can take place until these rituals have been observed. It is extremely rare for us to 'go straight to the point': even as we are saying that that is our intention, we are usually acknowledging that what has happened up to that moment was *not* the point.

Babies learn the first rudiments of social interaction a long time before they can actually utter anything that sounds like language.

Indeed, it is no exaggeration to say that this process starts at birth, since parents use the baby's various movements and noises to simulate the give-and-take of interactive conversation. C. E. Snow (1977) in an article on the development of conversation between mothers and babies quotes the following example of 'turn-taking' between a mother and her infant.

> MOTHER: Hello. Give me a smile then. (gently pokes infant in the ribs)
> INFANT: (yawns)
> MOTHER: Sleepy are you? You woke up too early today.
> INFANT: (opens fist)
> MOTHER: (touching infant's hand) What are you looking at? Can you see something?
> INFANT: (grasps mother's finger)
> MOTHER: Oh, that's what you wanted. In a friendly mood, then. Come on, give us a smile.

From the ages of three or four months, babies will respond to parental smiles and will also 'greet' their parents in this way in order to initiate interaction. Whole 'conversations' thus take place with a succession of actions and reactions, gurgles, cries, smiles and the like, teaching the child to take his turn in conversations. This behaviour is so fundamental to human communication that we rarely think of it as something we had to learn.

In the months preceding the time when they start producing words that can be recognised as such by their parents, babies produce a great variety of sounds, including many that do not exist in their parents' language or languages. This is perfectly normal and is, indeed, an absolutely essential phase in children's development. They are learning to control and use their vocal apparatus, and trying out all the different articulatory possibilities it allows, but not yet associating any of the noises so produced with particular meanings. Gradually, the range and number of sounds diminishes, largely because the parents' reactions favour and encourage some (that is, the sounds of their languages) rather than others, in a sort of whittling down process.

One of the main ways in which parents help children with this process of discovery and selection is by associating certain sounds with certain routines. The child who smiles back, plays 'boo', says 'Mummy and Daddy', 'thank you' and 'bye-bye' is learning the essentials of social routines – greeting, recognising, identifying, thanking, leave-taking and so on – which he will use throughout the rest of his life. V. Cook (1979) comments:

> My daughter Nicola . . . used to make a sort of 'eeyore' noise whenever she handed something to someone. It was some time before we realised that she was trying to say 'Here you are'. She had learnt that 'Here you are' is part of the routine for handing people things, even if her parents were hardly aware that this was so.

Similar routines are used by babies to attract their parents' attention, to get what they want, in other words, to serve all their social needs, even though they may be able to use only one 'word' at a time and even though these words might be far from sounding like 'proper' words.

1.2   Exchanging information

Babies very soon want to 'show and tell'. In fact, they usually start producing their 'first words' to name the people around them and the things which are important to them: Mummy, Daddy, bottle, biscuit, dog, and so on. They also name 'actions' and the results of actions, as when they say 'gone' after their mother has left the room or when their bottle or bowl is empty.

When a child uses only one-word utterances of this kind, it is very difficult to know exactly what he means or what he is trying to do. This means that parents are constantly guessing, repeating or elaborating on what they think baby is saying, and this is, in turn, the richest possible 'input' for the child, who uses it as raw material to develop his own language and intellect.

This exchange of information is not one-sided, though. Babies do more than just 'name' things mechanically for the sake of putting a label on them. They are also, it seems reasonable to guess, expressing interest in certain things they have noticed: after all, there are lots of things they do *not* name. They are, then, making critical comments on the world around them.

1.3   Thinking

The 'mistakes' children make when they start naming objects at this one-word stage reveal that they are beginning to make sense of the world around them. This is particularly obvious when the child uses one word to refer to two objects which have something in common, but which are usually given different names. When a child uses 'Daddy' for all male human beings, or 'doggy' for all four-legged animals, he is revealing that he has already classified animate beings along a number of dimensions which may not yet be the right ones, but which are none the less meaningful: 'doggies' are not to be confused with 'daddies'. It should not worry parents to find small children making even bigger 'mistakes' than this: they are just testing and learning the system. An eight-month-old girl notices a brass ornament and stretches out to touch it. Her parents recognise what it is she's after, and she learns the Swedish word for 'horse' *häst*. But the child's *häst* does not yet mean 'horse', as we see when she uses it first to indicate another object in which she is interested, next as a general attention-getter, then as something like 'pretty', before even beginning to put it into the 'animals' pigeon-hole.

A child learning a language is *learning about the world*, about how it is organised and how it works. This is very different, if only in degree, from the adult learning a second language, who tends to work the other way round: he brings his world with him and uses the language to try to express it. Moreover, as a result of their cognitive development, adults can use language in ways which are not available to young children; they are able to make conscious use of cognitive skills, for instance to solve complex problems or to plan a series of actions.

One of the greatest advantages of bilingualism is that even very small children realise that the relationship between words and the objects they refer to is not a necessary one, that the same things can have different names. It does seem that this early exercise in abstraction does give the bilingual the mental flexibility and openness which has frequently been reported by experimenters and psychologists. This flexibility in turn is one of the main protections against what monolinguals often imagine must be an unpleasant experience – thinking in two languages. Quite literally, the bilingual does not *mind* this. There are a number of reasons why this is so: first, there are thought processes that are non-verbal or pre-verbal anyway. Secondly, verbal thought – our 'interior monologue' – is usually conscious and the bilingual will *choose* which language to think in. Thirdly, many bilinguals are in the habit of always thinking in one language except when they are actually using another (our guess is that this is the majority). Fourthly, many bilinguals actually like being able to think in two languages, often using it as a creative approach to problem-solving, a sort of lateral thinking.

Unfortunately, this is one of those cases where 'if you have to ask the question, you may not understand the answer' and all the bilingual can do when he is asked what language he thinks in is to say 'Well, it depends . . .'

1.4 Playing with words

Babies and small children love playing with language. Before they can produce actual words, they will spend long stretches repeating the same sounds apparently just for fun. Children who can only say very few words will use them to sing themselves to sleep. Playing with sounds and words in this way seems to be a completely spontaneous activity in children; it is also an important part of the learning process and it is an activity which the child will continue to perform with various degrees of complexity, going from bad jokes to humming songs to writing poetry, throughout his adult life.

'Lullation', as this behaviour is sometimes called, serves much the same purposes, and gives the child much the same sort of pleasure, as do nursery rhymes and all sorts of verbal activities and games later on. Amongst the purposes there is obviously the learning through repetition of basic words, sounds and structures, but the high proportion of 'nonsense' – expressions like 'ring a ring of roses', 'Humpty Dumpty' and 'hey diddle diddle' – is surely there at least as much for the fun of it.

This point is more important to the parents of bilingual children than might at first seem to be the case, because some parents worry that it is a symptom of confusion, since naturally the bilingual child will call on both his repertoires to 'talk nonsense': in a sense it is, but it is also the process of getting it all sorted out. To put it another way, in what sense is: '*Beurre*, bird, butter, *beurre*' chanted dozens of times, inferior as word-play to: 'Hickory, dickory dock, the mouse ran up the clock' or: 'A tisket, a tasket, I've got a little basket', and in what sense is it more 'mixed' than such rhymes?

Far from being an alarm signal of any kind, verbal play of this kind should be seen as a healthy, normal stage for any child to pass through. Indeed, one might almost go as far as to say that it is in cases where the child does *not* do this sort of thing that the parents should start getting worried. Generalisations of this kind are dangerous, though, so for the moment we will limit ourselves to the observation that a very high proportion of the parents of productive bilinguals in our study mentioned an early period of mixing, which seems usually to have occurred between one and a half and three years of age. This 'statistic' must be taken with more than a pinch of salt: firstly because of the considerable variation between children in these matters, secondly because it is based on parents' recollections of how their child developed, not on any stricter form of observation.

1.5   Communicating while learning

From the moment a child reaches the 'two-word' stage his ability to express himself increases enormously and he starts producing utterances which look like adult sentences. He also becomes more efficient in his conversational routines and in exchanging information. Another important development is that he begins to indicate that things do *not* exist or that he does *not* want something, by putting 'no' in front of the names of objects.

However, at the beginning of this stage the child still makes no use of 'link words' ('to', 'off', 'the', 'and', 'if', etc.) nor does he put grammatical endings ('runs') at the end of words. These words and endings are gradually added during the years that follow: again, the time taken will depend to some extent on the individual child, but it also depends on the language in question. Some languages (for example, Finnish, Russian) have more word endings than others, so naturally children take longer to learn them. This does not mean that such languages are more difficult for children to learn, since all languages have roughly the same degree of complexity: but that complexity can be distributed differently, so a certain area of a given language *can* be more difficult than the same area in another language. This is another reason why bilingual children's development of their two languages can vary, in detail, quite considerably.

In English, the first ending to be learnt will usually be '-ing', as in 'Mummy coming'. This is followed by the genitive 's' as in 'Mummy's car' and then, much later, by the plural 's' as in 'cars'.

Perhaps more important, the child now learns that word order also varies and changes meanings. However, 'cracking the code' of word order will take him some time, during which he will make many 'mistakes'. In very general terms, the problem is one of aligning grammatical structures with possible meanings, of linking language with reality. For example, if he is presented with a toy dog and a doll and told 'Give the man the dog', he will give *the man to the dog* rather than *the dog to the man*, because in most sentences the noun which follows the verb is the person who receives something ('Penny gave John the book') and he has not yet learnt that in real life you usually give people pets and not vice versa.

Another area of difficulty related to word order is *questions*. Typically, children will start by using 'question words' such as 'where' and 'what', but without making the necessary changes in the order of the words which follow. For some time, they continue to produce sentences like: 'What time it is?'

As the child's language slowly develops, he also becomes a more sophis-ticated interactor. This is reflected in his use of pronouns: he starts calling his mother and father 'you', for example. This is an important step, since it shows that he is no longer limited to expressing *himself*, that he is now aware of the separate existence of others and can relate what he is saying to them. Indeed, it is fascinating to note that this development usually coincides with the time when the child turns his picture book the right way up when he wants to show it to someone: he has realised, quite literally, that there are other points of view.

Once the child has made this distinction between 'I' and 'the others', his personality begins to develop; he becomes more assertive when he plays with other children, but on the other hand he also starts cooperating with them. It is now that he starts playing with other children, his linguistic and social development going hand in hand, as will be seen if he attends some kind of playgroup. This is partly why children starting or consolidating a 'second' language under these circumstances invariably learn it so quickly, easily and well; their whole being is directed to that purpose at a time of maximum readiness and opportunity. They are not learning *about* the language, they are learning *in* the language through using it.

By the age of five or thereabouts, the majority of children have cleared the major hurdles of 'grammar', but will still make a number of errors. Here, as elsewhere, individual variation can be extraordinary – which is one reason why we have been careful not to state ages at which any of the phases we have discussed 'should' or 'will' be reached. The celebrated cases of Einstein, who did not speak till he was three, and of Runeberg who waited until he was four and then went on to become Finland's national poet, should not be interpreted as meaning that all children who do likewise will become great mathematicians or writers. But they are a useful reminder that parents do often worry unduly about their children 'not doing what the books say they should be doing at that age' when there is no cause for concern.

We will be returning in more detail to the development of the bilingual child in Chapter 4. For the moment, though, we are going to look at a number of basic ideas about language which might be helpful to parents trying to understand what it is that their child is learning.

Some general ideas about language

1.6   'Languages' and 'dialects'

There are between three and five thousand languages spoken in the world at present. The vagueness of this figure is due to the fact that there is no way of distinguishing between dialects and languages on linguistic grounds alone. We *all* speak a dialect and we *all* have accents. Moreover, linguistic boundaries only rarely coincide with political or geographical boundaries; if you start walking through France from Calais and go all the way to the southern tip of Italy, you will never find two adjacent villages where inhabitants do not understand one another, yet at some 'point' you will have gone from French to Italian. In fact, it is more accurate to say you will have gone from France to Italy, since the border is national and political, not linguistic.

Certain dialects, or groups of dialects, have greater prestige than others, and it is these which we usually refer to as 'languages'. But this prestige has nothing to do with the intrinsic qualities of the dialects in question. They are not more beautiful, more logical or older than the other dialects. Their prestige springs from their uses and their users. Such dialects are usually those spoken by the educated and the upper classes; they are the ones used in the official administration and education of the country; they have a written form and have been studied and standardised. The word 'language' is a social and political label we attach to a dialect that is officially recognised. This is why, when there is disagreement about the status of a dialect, the conflict is inevitably political in nature. For example, when people argue as to whether Breton, Scots or Basque is 'a language', they are usually arguing about the degree of political autonomy of the speakers or the region where the variety in question is spoken.

Because languages are not distinguished from dialects on linguistic grounds, it is quite possible to find separate official languages that have more in common than other dialects of the 'same' language. For example, we speak of the 'Scandinavian languages' – Norwegian, Danish and Swedish – even though they are very similar and often mutually comprehensible. On the other hand, we speak of 'dialects' of the Chinese language even though at least eight of these dialects (or rather families of dialects) are mutually incomprehensible. Words like 'Norwegian' and 'Chinese' are political, not linguistic statements: they tell us that the area in question is a separate nation. As it has often been said: 'a language is a dialect with an army and a navy of its own'.

In many places, people speak two dialects. When these are officially recognised as languages, we say that such people are 'bilingual', but in purely linguistic terms anyone who has two different forms of speech available is bilingual. When Philip Riley was a grammar-school boy in the London of the 1950s, he and his classmates received elocution lessons in Standard English and their cockney accents were frowned on at school, so that most of them spoke differently at home and at school. In the same way, the German businessman who 'puts on his regional accent with his slippers in the evening' is just doing what bilinguals do. This, again, is why it is so difficult to count languages, dialects and bilinguals: there are no clear dividing lines.

The four or five thousand languages of the world differ widely in the number of people who speak them. The average number of speakers per language is estimated to be one million. On the other hand, nations also differ widely in the number of languages spoken in them, the average being about thirty. The idea then, that each country has *one* language, spoken uniformly by all the people within its borders, is both naive and inaccurate, even though most countries do have a standard dialect or dialects, recognised as the official language or languages.

1.7   The written language and the spoken language

Speech is the primary form of language. It existed before there was any form of writing and children learn to speak before they learn to write.

Many languages are never written and many people never learn to read or write. Speech is fast and fleeting, writing relatively slow and permanent. Both forms have their advantages: speech is immediate, writing leaves a record. Because of the extra time and effort involved, we tend to use the written form for messages which are in some sense more important and to compose such messages more carefully. This does not, however, alter the primacy of the spoken form. Nor does it, therefore, make sense to judge speech by the criteria we use for writing. Anybody who really 'talks like a book' immediately strikes us as extremely odd.

Clearly, it is possible to be bilingual in both speech and writing. But it may also happen that a bilingual only learns to read and write in one of his two languages, usually the one he has been educated in.

1.8   Change

The very nature of the written medium makes it resistant to change: this is an advantage, as it enables later readers to 'consult the record' more easily. Speech changes considerably more rapidly (though, eventually, these changes will find their way into the written form, too). This is an advantage, as it allows the language to adapt to and to assimilate changes in the way of life of the people who speak it – new inventions, ideas, attitudes and relationships make new demands on the language. A language which cannot respond to these demands is a dead language; change is not, therefore, automatically change for the worse, it is a sign of life.

Most changes occur imperceptibly in our daily lives: we occasionally notice a new word or expression, but then it either drops out of circulation, or we learn it and forget that it was new. Even so, we are usually well aware that we do not speak quite like our parents did, and that our children speak somewhat differently from ourselves. Only if we return from a long stay abroad, or open an old book, does the rate of change really strike us: suddenly everybody seems to be saying 'absolutely' or 'wicked', or 'methinks' and 'thou'.

Change may occur at any level of a language. If you listen to recordings of BBC wartime news broadcasts now, you will realise just how much has changed as regards pronunciation, for example. It was argued at the time that if the news was read by a northerner or a woman no one would believe it. This shows that changes of this kind are often the expression of social developments. It is interesting to note, though, that the World Service of the BBC consistently uses announcers who have much more 'upper-class' accents than those used in the BBC's programmes produced for Britain.

1.9   Levels of language

Language is a complex phenomenon which has different levels of structure that correspond to different types of organisation. In outline, these are:

i)   Sound   The 'raw material' of language and how it is patterned in particular languages. The 'sounds' of English, Dutch, French, etc.

ii)   Grammar   The structure of words and the structures we make with words (that is, sentences).

iii)   Meaning   The literal meanings of sentences and the meanings of utterances in real-life situations.

Let us take each level for brief examination.

Sound

Each language uses only a small selection of the vast range of sounds that the human vocal tract can produce. Judgements as to the relative 'purity' or 'beauty' of these sounds are value judgements which may be subjectively real for speakers but which have no objective basis.

Pronunciation is not just a matter of articulating consonants and vowels in the right place and in the right manner. Other aspects of speech that involve more than single consonants or vowels, such as stress, length, tone and intonation, are just as important.

A speaker's pronunciation is an index of the social group to which he belongs, wishes to belong or perceives his interlocutor to belong. Our pronunciation varies far more than most of us realise according to the situation we find ourselves in, who we are talking to, whether we are speaking formally or not, rapidly or not and so on. Variations of this kind are not due to 'carelessness' or 'slovenly articulation'.

The relationship between sounds and meanings is, with a very few exceptions (words like 'cuckoo'), an arbitrary one.

Grammar

Every language has morphological rules for constructing words (we say 'farm-er' not 'er-farm', for example) and syntactic rules for constructing sentences. People learning a *second* language will have the impression that it is 'difficult' or 'easy' depending on its degree of correspondence with their first language.

There are no 'primitive' languages, in the sense of languages that are somehow incomplete or rudimentary. There are, of course, languages spoken by so-called 'primitive' peoples: but these are just as complex from the linguistic point of view as, say, Russian, Chinese or English.

There are no languages that 'don't have a grammar'. If this were so, communication would be impossible, since speakers and hearers need common rules to express and interpret their intentions: if there were no code at all there would not be any message. Indeed, if a language had no grammar, it would be impossible to learn it: there would be nothing to learn. However, not all grammars are of the same kind; in particular, we need to free ourselves from the idea that grammar is exclusively a matter of word endings or sentence construction. Relations between words (that is, grammatical rules) can be signalled in many other ways, including rhythm, tone and word order. For example, we often hear that 'English is easy' because 'it doesn't have much grammar' (here, 'word endings'). Compared to, say, German or Finnish, this is true. But does this really mean that English is 'simpler' in some absolute sense? Not a bit of it! In English, *word order* is extremely complex and signals many of the relations that word endings signal in other languages. Consider, for example, the following perfectly ordinary English sentence: 'Some of the striking lorry-drivers had driven four abreast up the M1'. Now try to alter the position of even one of the words in this sentence. You will find it extremely difficult to do so without changing the meaning. It would be ungrammatical: and a rule that insists on twelve items appearing in one and only one order is an immensely complex one.

The use of English as an international language is not, therefore, the result of its 'simplicity' or, indeed, of any other intrinsic virtue. It is the result of historical developments which in themselves are almost entirely unrelated to language. What is true of English *vis-à-vis* other languages is equally true of the dialects and varieties of English: they derive their status and prestige, or their lack of it, from their functions, their uses and their users, and not from any inherent qualities. It is of great practical value to have a standard form of a language, such as 'Standard English', but from a purely linguistic point of view any other dialect would serve just as well: Standard English is not inherently superior in any way, only different. Its status is derived from the fact that it is the dialect of the upper classes (Oxford and Cambridge, the Court, the City, professional associations, and so on) and if they had spoken in any other way, *that* would be Standard English now. The objective historical factors determining the selection and emergence of a standard language do not in any way detract from its value and importance as the major form of access to knowledge and to certain social domains.

Meaning

The 'real' meaning of a word or expression is not restricted to its historical or etymological meaning, words mean what people use them to mean – not necessarily what they *used* to mean. To insist that the 'real' meaning of 'enthusiastic', for example, is 'to be inspired by a god' is either pedantry or a failure to understand what people who use the word nowadays are trying to convey.

Again, the same word usually has a number of different meanings. Only scientifically defined terms such as H_2O have a single unambiguous meaning; 'water', on the other hand, can mean a number of different things: 'He watered the garden', 'His mouth watered', 'The proposition was watered down' and so on. We are able to select the appropriate meaning because there are usually a number of other clues in what is said to help us, and because the context often narrows down the range of possible meanings.

We need to distinguish between the meaning that words and sentences have in use, and the meaning they have when they are not in use. The meaning of words in dictionaries or of sentences in grammars is only a part of the meaning they may have when spoken in real life. The relationship between what we *say* and what we *mean* is neither direct nor simple. A sentence like 'You are not going out' will have one meaning in a grammar book (its literal or semantic meaning) but in a situation it can be used to perform a wide variety of communicative acts. For example:

> *prohibition* (FATHER TO CHILD): 'You've got a cold and it's raining, so I forbid you to go out.'
> *request for confirmation* (WIFE TO HUSBAND): 'I have to go out myself: you will be in if Fred calls, won't you?'
> *threat* (KIDNAPPER TO VICTIM): 'If you try to move, I'll shoot you!'
> *reproach* (FATHER TO DAUGHTER): 'You've been down the pub every night this week!'

Learning *functional* uses of language of this kind is crucial: language is not just a system for conveying 'neutral' information (such as the fact that you are not going out) which is either true or false but nothing more. We also use it to *do* things, like prohibiting, threatening, inviting, agreeing, defining, greeting, persuading and ordering. We use it to express our feelings, to socialise, to play, to clarify our thoughts, all of which activities involve types of meaning that will not be found in dictionaries or grammars but which, to the speaker, are far more important than the meanings we do find there.

There are other kinds of meaning that occur in real-life interaction but not in dictionaries and grammars. The most important of these is meaning which is based on *common knowledge* of the way our world is organised. For example, in the exchange:

> A: I must get going or I'll miss my bus.
> B: It's half past eleven.

only shared knowledge about the bus-timetable (for example, the time of the last bus) will enable A to know whether B means: 'You have already missed it' or: 'You have plenty of time to catch it'. It is, of course, perfectly possible for two people to speak the same language without sharing the same knowledge in every detail. Every time we meet someone from another family, profession or town we have to provide the relevant information: 'Oh dear, the last bus was at eleven, I'm afraid you'll have to take a taxi'.

This is important from the point of view of the bilingual: he speaks the language but, perhaps because he has been living abroad, does not know many of the things that people who speak that language usually know. He may well have problems understanding what people mean that have nothing to do with the language as such, but with the way of life that is unfamiliar to him. Precisely because he speaks the language so well people will take it for granted that he knows things that he does not know but which they *would* expect to have to explain to a foreigner.

Finally, it is worth pointing out that there is no basis for the belief that certain languages are more logical or precise than others. The logic of natural languages like Norwegian or Spanish should not be confused with the logic of logicians, mathematicians and philosophers. The grammatical structure of a language is not such an 'objective' logical system, though the speakers of that language may believe it to be one, especially if they are monolinguals.

1.10   Varieties of language

Language varies over the centuries, it varies geographically, and it also varies from situation to situation. We do not speak in the same way in all situations, for example, in a law court, a bar, at church, on the phone, at work, at a football match or to our friends, doctors, husbands, wives, bosses and children. A language cannot be accounted for by a uniform set of rules that are always valid and always applied in the same way. Using a language involves a *wide range of activities* that are governed by social conventions and the social context in which the participants find themselves. To use an analogy, language is not a sport like cricket with its rule book, where all the players are engaged in the same game; it is more like an athletics meeting where sprints and relay races, marathons, jumping, putting the shot and all sorts of other 'events', each with its own nature and rules, may take place as part of the same 'meeting'.

Moreover, just as it is possible to be a champion hurdler without being any good at all at the 5,000 metres, so language users may be better at some linguistic events than others: and no one is ever equally good at everything, since training, personal gifts and preferences and opportunities are not the same for everybody.

The rules of each language event vary according to the nature of the activity: whether the medium is speech or writing, the roles of the participants, their relationships, their functions and intentions and so on. This means that every speaker has a number of different 'styles' that he changes according to the situation. To apply the same set of rules to all situations (for example, to insist that only Standard English is 'correct' or that one should always use a very formal style) is symptomatic of an inability to grasp just how much we vary in our linguistic behaviour from one situation to another and how much this variation is responsible for the flexibility of language, which enables us to use it for computer programs, advertisements, poetry, business deals and so on. 'Styles' may be different as regards pronunciation, vocabulary and grammar. The skills involved in choosing and employing an appropriate style are exactly the same as those employed by the bilingual when he chooses and employs the language appropriate to a particular situation. There is no difference between the child who learns when to say: 'Wotcher!' or 'Good morning', the child who learns when to say: *Salut!* ('Hi!') or *Bonjour* ('Good morning') and the child who learns when to say: 'Good morning' or *Bonjour*. In a very real sense, we are *all* bilinguals: each time we choose between two different forms to express the same idea, for example: 'Hello, Charlie, nice to see you' instead of: 'Good morning, Mr Brown', we are doing exactly what the bilingual does when he chooses between his two languages.

1.11   Acquiring a language

With the exception of a severely handicapped minority, all children learn at least one language. This has led many linguists to believe that the ability to learn a language is at least partly due to genetic programming which is specific to the human race: certainly, there is no other species that has anything like our communicative capabilities. This hypothesis is supported by the fact that children show a remarkable uniformity in their linguistic development: they go through a number of stages at predictable ages and the order in which they acquire the various structures and functions of language is also highly regular. Of course, this apparently innate capacity to learn a language is not restricted to any particular language (that of our parents, for example): a Vietnamese child brought to France and adopted at birth will learn French, not Vietnamese, and will go through the various stages of development which all French children go through. We may all be equipped at birth to learn a language, but we still have to learn it *from* someone, that is, from the members of the community in which we live.

At first, our circle of acquaintances is very limited: mother, father and possibly a few relatives. It is during this period that the parental role is most crucial, linguistically speaking, though it remains important for a number of years to come. As a child's world expands, he begins to meet more people, and to learn from them. Now it is other children who play the most important role in the child's development. For we are never taught to speak our mother tongue in any formal way (though later at school we may learn a considerable amount *about* it, which is not the same thing at all).

The mechanisms of this process of language acquisition are the subject of intense controversy and debate at present. In very general terms, the argument is between the 'structuralists', who believe that a child builds his own grammar, that is, a series of rules which are generalisations based on what he hears around him, and the 'functionalists', who believe that the community provides the child with meanings, which the child then relates to the language. At the risk of trivialising what is a technical and philosophically important discussion, one could say that the structuralists see the child as learning a code (rules which he can then use to create and transmit messages) whilst the functionalists see the child as a messenger whose main interest is in the effects produced by different kinds of message (which he can then use as a basis for cracking the code).

Despite these differences, there are a certain number of points concerning the learning process about which there is now a general consensus. Since several of these are in complete contradiction with what the person in the street thinks about learning, it is worth listing them briefly here.

First, a few points about what learning is *not*:

- *Learning a language is not simply a matter of repetition.* In fact repetition seems to play only a small and relatively superficial part in the learning process. This seems to be because language is systematic *and* dynamic: we can only repeat a part of the system, not the system itself. Moreover, if learning a language were merely a matter of repetition, how could we ever produce a sentence we had never heard before?

- *Correcting and being corrected does not have any great influence on the language learning process.* This is shown by the fact that we sometimes learn things straight away without ever being corrected and sometimes go on making the same old mistake, no matter how often we are corrected. When a child produces an incorrect but true utterance, such as 'mummy spoon', the mother usually does not correct the child but agrees with him, for instance by saying: 'Yes dear, what a good boy you are!' On the contrary, when a child says something which is grammatically well-formed, but which is not true, his mother will disagree. For instance, the child may say: 'This is Mummy's spoon' to which the mother will reply: 'No, of course not, it belongs to Daddy'. In fact, children are very often corrected for producing grammatical utterances and find themselves encouraged for producing errors. For this reason, it has been said that if learning was a simple matter of correction and encouragement, we should become adults who tell the truth ungrammatically, but of course, we tell lies . . . grammatically!

- *Learning is not a neat, linear process.* It is not like laying a single railway line across an open plain. Instead, it involves wrong turnings, meanders, shunting backwards and forwards, forgetting and remembering. We may take a perfectly correct route, only to find that there is an obstacle across the line: when we go back on our tracks, either to fetch something, to remove the obstacle or to find a different way round it, an outside observer may interpret our behaviour as 'a mistake', although we are, in fact, solving a problem.

- *Errors are not necessarily a sign of failure to learn.* They are an essential part of the learning process. When we come to a junction, we may well take a wrong turning but this helps us work out which was the right one. Errors are very often a healthy symptom that learning is taking place: the child who says: 'I goed' has learnt an extremely powerful rule for the formation of the past tense in English. He has not, though, yet learnt that the verb 'to go' is, in this respect, irregular.

Now a few points about what learning *is*:

- *Learning is an increase of the range of meanings that are available to an individual.* Only activities that are in themselves meaningful provide worthwhile opportunities for learning. Even the most 'superficial' aspects of a language, such as the difference, say, between the 'm' and 'n' sounds, are learnt in terms of the meaningful oppositions that they produce, such as 'mice' and 'nice'. This is even more so at the 'higher' or more 'complex' levels of language.
- *Learning a language is not the same thing as learning about a language.* Just as it is possible to be an expert on the grammar of German without actually speaking German, so it is possible to speak German fluently without having any idea of its grammar. Any *explicit* idea, that is: all speakers of German 'know' German grammar by definition. To say that only grammarians 'know' the grammar of a language is like saying that only doctors have bodies.
- *Learning is the product of 'motivation + opportunity'.* Small children do not usually need any encouragement to learn their language, but they may well need to be given the opportunity. Being cooped up on the twenty-first floor of a high-rise tower block in front of a TV screen is not the *rich interactional and linguistic environment* that a child needs if he is to master the full range of functions and styles of his mother tongue or tongues. On the other hand, hanging out with the neighbourhood gang might expose the child to a very wide range of words and functions.
- *Language is a social phenomenon and language learning is therefore a social activity.* There are many aspects of language use which can *only* be learnt in direct, face-to-face interaction with a wide variety of partners.

This last point leads us to conclude on the differences between *learning a language at home and learning a language at school.* The contrast between language learning at school and at home has perhaps been exaggerated. Indeed, research (Wells, 1981) has shown that evidence for the continuity between the two is much stronger than was thought before. There are differences, however:

- The school social context makes children familiar with interaction that is pedagogically motivated, in contrast with the multiplicity of goals underlying interactions at home, and also familiarises them with the requirements of conversation involving many participants, in contrast with smaller numbers at home.

– The school also provides the systematic training that helps develop higher levels of symbolic functioning associated in particular with the teaching of reading and writing, which contrasts with the spontaneous, untaught acquisition of speech at home.

Having said that, it is obvious that there is constant interaction between the two learning contexts of school and home. The wider the range of activities and skills developed at school, the more likely that they will be used beyond the confines of the classroom. This is obviously good news for the parents of bilingual children. Absence of formal training in one of the languages is not necessarily detrimental to the development of that language, if such continuity is fostered by the parents at home.

CHAPTER TWO

What is bilingualism?

2.1   Some definitions of bilingualism

If you ask people in the street what 'bilingual' means, they will almost certainly reply that it is being able to speak two languages 'perfectly'. Unfortunately, we cannot even describe exactly what speaking *one* language perfectly involves. No one speaks the whole of the English language: for example, do you know what 'stubs to can wall penetration welds' are? Or what 'tort' is? Or a 'treble top'? Probably not, unless you happen to be a welder, a lawyer or a darts player, and the chances of your being all three are almost non-existent. Each of us speaks *part* of our mother tongue. The bilingual does, too, that is, she speaks parts of two languages, and they very rarely coincide exactly. If she is a lawyer, for example, she may work only in English in her office or in court, but speak French at home, with the result that her legal English is far better (as such) than her legal French, and her domestic French is far better (as such) than her domestic English. How can we compare the two then? All we can say is that they are different tools for different purposes.

This problem, the fact that it is almost impossible to compare an individual's abilities in two different languages because we are not measuring the same things, is central to all discussion of bilingualism, and shows why the person in the street's 'definition' just will not do, except in very rare circumstances. It also explains why so many different definitions of bilingualism exist and why, though each may be a valid statement about one type of bilingualism, none is satisfactory or exhaustive.

Here, then, are some of the definitions which researchers and linguists have suggested. But don't be surprised to find them contradictory or too narrow.

> Bilingualism [is] native-like control of two languages . . . Of course, one cannot define a degree of perfection at which a good foreign speaker becomes a bilingual: the distinction is relative.   (L. Bloomfield, 1933)

> Bilingualism is understood . . . to begin at the point where the speaker of one language can produce complete, meaningful utterances in the other language.   (E. Haugen, 1953)

> The phenomenon of bilingualism [is] something entirely relative . . . We shall therefore consider bilingualism as the alternate use of two or more languages by the same individual.   (W. F. Mackey, 1962)

> The bilingual or wholistic view of bilingualism proposes that the bilingual is an integrated whole which cannot easily be decomposed into two separate parts. The bilingual is NOT the sum of two complete or incomplete monolinguals; rather, he or she has a unique and specific linguistic configuration.   (F. Grosjean, 1992)

> Bilingualism refers to the phenomenon of competence and communication in two languages . . . A bilingual society is one in which two languages are used for communication. In a bilingual society, it is possible to have a large number of monolinguals . . . provided that there are enough bilinguals to perform the functions requiring bilingual competence in that society. There is, therefore, a distinction between individual bilingualism and societal bilingualism.   (A. Lam, 2001)

Even the briefest of examinations of these quotations shows the importance of distinguishing between bilingual *societies* and bilingual *individuals*. Theoretically, it is quite possible to have a bilingual society in which all individual members speak only one language, just as it is possible to have a bilingual individual in an otherwise monolingual society. Secondly, these quotations underline the importance of the *relative* nature of bilingualism. At what point do we decide that someone is a bilingual? The fact that we can ask this question shows that the decision is to a large extent arbitrary.

In this chapter, we shall look at bilingualism from the point of view of society at large. The following chapter will focus on individual bilingualism and the meaning of growing up bilingually.

2.2   'Elitist' bilingualism and 'folk' bilingualism

Figures for 'intermarriages' in the EU countries are not easy to come by, but there is no doubt that in the last two decades there has been a considerable increase. Such parents are faced with a long-term choice, but there are at least two other categories of parents who, whilst their stay abroad may be much shorter, feel this problem just as acutely in the short term. These are parents who are abroad temporarily for educational or business purposes. Every year, about 12,000 students from the British Isles undertake extended residence abroad in the context of a degree programme and many post-graduates and research students go abroad as well. Moreover, the rise of the big multinationals intensifies this trend: In the 1980s, IBM alone employed some 20,000 people throughout Europe, of whom 6,000 worked at least some of the time in a foreign country.

If we have stressed the numbers of people concerned with this problem, it is partly to show that bilingualism of this kind is in no sense rare, partly to make the point that the parents involved are by no means all people who can afford private nannies and governesses or the fees of private or international schools. They are likely, it is true, to be middle-class professionals, but this does not mean that their problems are somehow less real than those of, say, guest-workers' families or people living in linguistic enclaves.

We feel that this needs to be emphasised because the sort of bilingualism we are discussing is often referred to as 'elitist' bilingualism which makes it sound as though those concerned are both small in number and rich. We ourselves, in discussions with colleagues, have often been given the impression that they thought we were wasting our time on the imaginary troubles of a pampered minority. As Tokuhama-Espinosa's study (2001) shows, bilingual and multilingual families now come from a much broader spectrum than ever before and as we hope we have shown, the teachers, soldiers, secretaries, business people, translators, technicians and so on who are now criss-crossing Europe are certainly relatively privileged when compared with most migrant communities, but to talk about them as if they are rich, with the implication that their riches can automatically solve their linguistic problems, is neither helpful nor accurate.

None the less, the distinction encapsulated in the 'elitist' / 'folk' opposition *is* a real one. *Elitist bilingualism* has been described as:

> The privilege of middle-class, well-educated members of most societies.
>
> (Paulston, 1975)

Folk bilingualism results from:

> The conditions of ethnic groups within a single state who have to become bilingual involuntarily, in order to survive. (Tosi, 1982)

Tosi comments:

> The distinction is a crucial one, as it shows that whilst the first group uses the education system which they control to seek bilingualism, the second group has bilingualism foisted upon it by an education system which is controlled by others. Research findings are also consistent in showing that privileged children from the dominant group do well academically whether they are educated in their mother tongue or in a second language.

Whilst the 'elitist' / 'folk' opposition is a valid distinction, the idea that middle-class foreigners somehow manipulate the educational system of the host country to their own advantage is too simplistic. Perhaps the concept of *elective bilingualism* would be more appropriate here. It has sometimes been used to refer to forms of bilingualism where the acquisition of the second language is a matter of choice for the parents more than an absolute necessity brought about by economic or political circumstances. In fact, our own experiences in dealing with the French and English systems showed us just how helpless the individual can be when dealing with monolithic institutions.

Most families who face the problem are in fact left to their own devices, and find themselves faced with a number of problems:

– The management of 'elitist bilingualism' in bilingual homes is not as easy as it looks and no sources of advice are available. We keep meeting a great variety of couples who would certainly be labelled 'middle-class' in sociological surveys but who are at a complete loss as to how to go about maintaining two languages in their family.
– In a number of cases, the language concerned is *not* a 'high-status foreign language' which means that even if the family in question were well-off they would still not be able to shift the responsibility for maintaining that language to a private institution, such as an international school, since such schools naturally concentrate on 'majority' languages.
– Most such families will, therefore, send their children to the local state schools. In many cases, they find that the modern language curriculum is inadequate for their children's needs. For instance, in Great Britain, a French / English bilingual family will discover to their amazement that it is almost impossible to find a state secondary school that offers anything but French as a first foreign language for an eleven year old. Their child, perfectly fluent in French, will be refused the opportunity of learning any other foreign language in the first form and will have to attend French classes with children who are absolute beginners in that language.

– This polarisation between the privileged ones and the rest hides a real problem, and one that is common to *both* groups: if bilingualism is not maintained, it means that somewhere along the line, someone will lose his/her linguistic identity – and it is usually the mother.

A bilingual upbringing and education can be highly successful and it is not dangerous in itself. But many parents, faced with problems like those mentioned above, influenced by ill-founded advice, and in the absence of any source of encouragement or practical instructions, simply give up. This often results in a deep sense of loss for one of the parents, and has unfortunate social and practical repercussions, such as the children's being unable to communicate with their grandparents. We believe that this is a pity. There can obviously be no question of forcing bilingualism on people who do not want it, but at least parents should be helped to make an informed choice, for or against; and if they choose for, straightforward advice should be given.

2.3   Different kinds of bilingual societies

In this book we concentrate on bilingual individuals and not bilingual societies, so this section will be kept as short as possible. It is important, though, to have some idea as to the reasons why whole societies can be bi- or multilingual, since individual bilingualism is usually the result of the same sort of pressures, only on a much smaller scale.

Bilingual societies often develop when different language groups come into contact for economic and commercial reasons, as in the case of Spanish-speaking Mexico and the English-speaking USA.

In certain countries, bilingualism exists in those areas where linguistic minorities are present, usually as a result of historical and political changes, such as a re-drawing of national borders. Alsace is a case in point: most speakers of Alsatian also speak French.

In other countries, bilingualism is more widespread. In Tanzania, for example, Swahili is the medium of instruction in primary schools for children speaking one of ten different Bantu languages or Maasai (a non-Bantu language spoken in the north-east of the country).

One particular form of social bilingualism is referred to as *diglossia* (Ferguson, 1959). In very general terms indeed, this means that the language used on formal occasions, for official purposes and for writing, usually referred to as 'high' forms, differs from that used in ordinary everyday conversation, referred to as 'low' forms. Since this is true of any language to some degree (we would not usually open a letter in English with the words: 'Hello, Charlie, how's things?'), this is obviously another very relative statement. The two forms may only be slightly different, in which case we would probably refer to them as a 'standard' and a 'dialect', or they might be completely separate languages. Where we come across references to 'high' and 'low' forms or to 'classical' or 'standard' languages, we can usually be sure that we are dealing with some form of diglossia. This form of societal bilingualism is far more common than is generally realised: both Arabic- and Greek-speaking countries exhibit it, for example, as does the German part of Switzerland. The relationship between individual bilingualism and diglossia is an immensely complex one, since it is quite possible to use only the high or low forms, or both, or one better than the other, and since the factors that determine the individual's linguistic identity may well be a compound of historical, geographical, ethnic, religious, economic and psychological influences.

In huge and diverse countries like the USA and the Community of Independent States, the present linguistic and ethnic compositions of the populations result from different types of colonising processes. In America:

> Many different people were attracted from many parts of the world. An intensive process of ethnic and linguistic convergence resulted and the colonial movement is centripetal. In Europe, the process has been one of divergence: the colonial process is centrifugal.   (G. Lewis, 1981)

Both countries have large groups of bilinguals, but as the result of very different social and political developments.

Bilingualism may be essentially an urban phenomenon, as in Madina (in Ghana) where most inhabitants speak three languages, or New York's El Barrio (Zentella, 1997), while elsewhere it may be characteristic of a mainly rural society, as in New Guinea.

There is a tendency for certain trades to be associated with bilingualism. Many builders in northern France, who are of Italian origin, are speakers of Italian, for example. Then there are those occupations that directly involve the daily use of several languages: translating and interpreting, of course, but also the diplomatic service, certain branches of the IT software industry and the travel and tourist industries, communications, journalism and teaching.

Finally, it is worth noting that bilingualism has often been the hallmark of the upper classes. Probably the best-known example of this is that of the

Russian aristocracy, who learnt French as a 'second mother tongue'. In *War and Peace* the main characters often switch from Russian to French.

2.4   Bilingualism is not rare

Over half the world's population is bilingual. This fact is usually surprising to many Europeans, who are under the impression that living with two or more languages is exceptional. It runs counter to popular views of the relationship between language and national or individual identity (see section 2.5) according to which one person speaks one language and all speakers of that language belong to the same country. Yet a little reflection shows that the predominance of bilingualism, at least at the national level, must necessarily be the case: however problematic this kind of figure might be, it is estimated that there are about 6,000 languages in the world today (Crystal, 1997) but there are only about 150 countries to fit them all into.

Of course, it is also true that languages do not all have the same numerical importance. Chinese (if counted as a single language, which is debatable) is spoken by 1,000 million people, or close to a quarter of the world's population, whilst other languages only have a handful of speakers; in the late 1960s it was reported that one North American Indian language was 'now only spoken by two elderly sisters who use it when they happen to meet'.

Again, languages can have very different geographical distributions. French is spoken as a native language in several countries (Belgium, Switzerland, Canada) whereas others may occupy only a fraction of a country: Scots Gaelic, for instance, is largely restricted to the Scottish Highlands and the Inner and Outer Hebrides.

However, even when we have allowed for these facts and however approximate this kind of counting might be, it is clear that most countries must be shared by speakers of different languages and that, in consequence, the number of people who use two or more languages must be correspondingly high. In simple, 'evolutionary' terms, it is most unlikely that bilingualism could continue to exist on this scale if there were anything intrinsically disadvantageous in it.

2.5   National identity and the monolingual state: the example of France, French and the French

France is often cited as the clearest example of the modern nation state and it is true that the degree of centralisation there surpasses that of any other Western European country; Paris and its suburbs houses almost a fifth of the country's population in just over two per cent of its total surface area. The uniformity of the educational system and the existence of regulatory bodies such as the *Académie Française* give a first impression of linguistic harmony and order.

Yet this monolingualism is a recent development, and is essentially a by-product of the centralising process. The provincial dialects of France were not mutually intelligible with the speech of Paris until the eighteenth century. Only with the coming of the French Revolution did this all change. At first, the Constituent Assembly decided to have all laws translated into the local dialects, but the Jacobin Convention which followed reversed this decision. They argued that linguistic diversity had been maintained intentionally by the Old Régime in order to keep the privileged classes, who spoke the Paris dialect, in power. They decided to impose linguistic uniformity to achieve linguistic equality, and this has been the conscious policy of French governments ever since: speakers of minority languages or dialects must be obliged to speak French for their own good. In the words of the Abbé Grégoire, who had been made responsible for implementing a questionnaire to provide information about local dialects:

> Feudalism preserved this variety of dialects to strengthen further the chains which bound the serfs. If our liberty is to be maintained, they must be abolished . . . The consistent use of the language of freedom must be imposed as soon as possible if the republic is to be united and undivided.
> (Report on the necessity of and the methods for destroying *patois* and making the use of French universal, 6 June 1789 – republished in Grégoire, 1999)

This policy has been pursued for over two centuries and French is indeed now spoken the length and breadth of the country. But have 'these jargons which are the tattered remnants of feudalism and slavery' disappeared? In 1976, Valdman estimated that 'the number of persons in France who have a passive knowledge and some active mastery of a local language not directly related to French', that is, persons who are to some degree bilingual in Basque, Breton, Alsatian, Flemish, Catalan, Corsican and Occitan, is approximately nine million. And this in the most 'uniformly monolingual country in Europe'!

Overall, if one adds the estimated two million migrant workers from Portugal and North Africa, we find that over twenty per cent of the present population of France is bilingual. In spite of this, the French language is still felt to represent and enhance the unity of the nation – the recognition of local languages being only a compromise. To date, and in spite of the repeated recommendations of successive ministers of education, the French government has not ratified the European Charter of Regional Languages. Even this degree of recognition is regarded (by French mono-linguals, obviously) as a danger, undermining national unity, and every-thing possible is done to present the *langues locales* as museum pieces:

> The whole of the French national heritage including not only historic monuments, but regional languages and cultures, ought to be preserved ... Regional diversity should strengthen national unity, though. There can be no question of it sapping, still less of it undermining that unity.
>
> (J. Chirac, 'France's Linguistic Problems', *Le Monde*, 7 February 1975)

In the light of what was said above, it seems only fitting that the author of those lines later became Mayor of Paris, Prime Minister and then President of the French Republic!

The relevance of this point to the type of family bilingualism we are dis-cussing in this book may not seem immediately obvious. The point is, though, that we have met many parents who fear a disruptive effect on the community of their family. Some of them, therefore, suppress their own linguistic identity and settle for, at most, a programme of cultural informa-tion about the country of origin.

2.6   'Official' and individual bilingualism

The fact that a nation is *officially* bilingual is not usually a good guide to the proportion of its citizens who are bilingual. As Grosjean (1982) has pointed out:

> Many so-called monolingual countries have a high percentage of speakers who use two or more languages on a regular basis, whereas many multilin-gual countries have rather few bilinguals.

Officially monolingual nations

These would include France (see above), Germany, or Japan (Yamamoto, 2001), where the official language is the mother tongue of most of the inhabitants, but where in fact there are considerable numbers of bilin-gual individuals from old or more recent minority groups. There are also officially monolingual countries like Tanzania or Indonesia, where one official language has been chosen as a lingua franca for a multilingual society.

Officially bilingual nations

These are nations like Canada, Belgium or Finland, where two or more languages have full official recognition, one of the languages being invariably that of a minority group. But this certainly does not mean that all of the individual inhabitants of the countries are bilingual:

> In fact, there are fewer bilingual people in the bilingual countries than there are in the so-called unilingual countries. For it is not always realized that bilingual countries were created not to promote bilingualism, but to guarantee the maintenance and use of two or more languages in the same nation. (Mackey, 1967)

Grosjean gives the example of officially bilingual Canada where only 13 per cent of the population uses both French and English on a regular basis, whereas in officially monolingual Tanzania, some 90 per cent of the population regularly uses at least two languages. Again, in officially bilingual Finland, only about six per cent of the population is (officially) bilingual.

Officially multilingual nations

Either they are countries like Switzerland, where the main national languages are all recognised as official languages, or they are countries like India, which have a large number of national languages only some of which are recognised as official languages for practical purposes: of the fourteen national languages mentioned in the constitution, only Hindi and English are official languages (Srivastava, 1988). The inhabitants of bilingual and multilingual countries are not themselves automatically bi- or multilingual. In India 'only about ten per cent of the population uses two languages regularly' (Grosjean, 1982).

It is important to realise, then, that official labels like 'monolingual', 'bilingual', or 'multilingual' have little to do with the actual distribution of bilingualism. Such labels are better understood as political statements of attitude towards minority groups rather than as statistical indications of the degree of bilingualism amongst the country's inhabitants. This is why, in Western Europe, the questions raised by the education of the children of linguistic minorities can only be dealt with at the level of official policy and planning within society as a whole, whereas for the many isolated cases of the sort we are dealing with here, it is largely a matter of negotiation and support *within the family unit.*

We will now proceed directly to a consideration of what it means to live in a bilingual situation and how different family contexts can affect a child's type of bilingualism.

CHAPTER THREE

....

Some things you should know about being bilingual

3.1 Bilingualism is a matter of degree

Everybody knows what 'bilingual' means; yet, as we have seen, as soon as we start trying to define the concept precisely, things get very complicated. This is not just hair splitting; if bilingualism is complex, it is because it is directly related to complex social issues.

Most definitions run into trouble because they derive from a view of bilingualism that is *idealised*. The bilingual is regarded as 'someone who speaks two languages perfectly'. For example, in the quotation from Bloomfield given above (section 2.1) we found him referring to bilingualism as 'native-like control of two languages'. But what *is* 'native-like control'? We only have to look around us to see that people vary enormously in the degree to which they can control their native language, and exactly the same is true for the non-native. At what point, then, do we decide that he is now 'native-like'? As Bloomfield continues:

> Of course, one cannot define a degree of perfection at which a good foreign speaker becomes a bilingual: the distinction is relative.

This is not a contradiction, but a realisation that bilingual people have to be placed on a continuum relative to the notion of 'native-like control' of two languages. In other words, the problem is that of defining *degrees of bilingualism*. Bilingualism is not a black-and-white, all-or-nothing phenomenon; it is a more-or-less one. We recognise this every time we say that: 'Fred speaks better German than Joe'.

However, just as it is hard to think of people who really have achieved total mastery of two languages in every possible domain, so it is difficult

33

to go to the opposite extreme and say like Haugen that 'bilingualism is understood ... to begin at the point where the speaker of one language can produce complete meaningful utterances in the other language'. It may well be the 'beginning' of the process, but it is not useful as a definition, since millions of people are able to do just that, yet never make any further progress and never reach the point where anybody would want to call them 'bilingual'. The imbalance between the two languages is so great that to say the speaker is bilingual would simply not be useful.

A different approach to bilingualism is to be found in the works of those linguists who see it not in terms of *relative competence* ('He speaks Swedish and Italian equally well') but in terms of *relative use* ('He speaks Swedish and Italian every day'). Mackey (1962) refers to 'the alternate use of two or more languages by the same individual', whilst Weinreich (1953) speaks of 'the practice of alternatively using two languages'. Such definitions do beg a number of questions, such as what we mean by 'using' a language, but they also have the advantage of leaving room for manoeuvre, of not excluding those kinds of bilingualism which are not 'perfect'. Since, in their daily lives, bilinguals use two languages, they are often difficult to label: depending on what they do in which language, their relationship with the people they talk to and the kinds of things they talk about, their pattern of bilingualism varies enormously. Consider the following examples. Friederike, a German student, has lived in England for a number of years. Back in Germany, she goes to her bank and asks to see the manager to discuss various matters. Suddenly she realises that she is having trouble expressing herself because she has never conducted this kind of conversation in German before. George, an English / French adolescent, is mad on chess. He lives in England, and has always played for his local club. Whilst on holiday in Spain, he meets a French boy and they start talking in French, about their hobbies and interests. The new friend turns out to be a chess player too, at which point George realises that he simply doesn't know how to talk about chess in French.

Although such problems are usually short-lived (indeed, most bilinguals acquire very efficient communication strategies for dealing with them) they do arise frequently. There are 'chunks' of life that the bilinguals have only experienced in one or other of their languages: although they do not usually have any problem understanding what is said by others on these topics (provided they have the requisite 'outside' knowledge, such as the rules of chess) they find that the appropriate words simply do not come to them when they wish to say something on the topic in question themselves.

In such circumstances, the words that do come to their lips are those belonging to the other language. This is the phenomenon known as *interference*, which has been defined as:

> Those deviations from the norms of either language which occur in the speech of bilinguals as a result of their familiarity with more than one language. (Weinreich, 1953)

A typical example is that of Monique, a Frenchwoman living in England, whose entire experience of 'motherhood' has been acquired exclusively in English. Speaking to a French friend on the phone, Monique chatted happily about her baby's *bouteilles* ('bottles', instead of *biberons*) until her friend began to ask just how much wine the infant was getting through. It is worth noting that this kind of error would probably not have appeared in a *written* vocabulary test designed to 'measure' the balance between her two languages, but that none the less this sort of error crops up in conversation.

Interference can occur at any level of language structure or function. For example, when it occurs at the phonetic level, it gives rise to a 'foreign accent'. An English dominant English / French bilingual may pronounce 'd' and 't' in the English way, with his tongue a little bit above and behind the teeth rather than with typical French dental articulation.

At the level of vocabulary, interference usually manifests itself by a failure to choose correctly between related words. For example, a French dominant French / English bilingual may say: 'I went to the library this morning', instead of 'I went to the bookshop'. Similarly, a Swedish dominant Swedish / English bilingual might say: 'He's in my bad papers' for 'He's in my bad books'.

It is also possible for the grammatical structures of one language to interfere with those of another. A common enough example of this is the ordering of words according to the rules of the dominant language, as when an English dominant English / French bilingual says: '*C'est celui que je parlais avec*' for '*C'est celui avec lequel je parlais*', under the influence of the English structure: 'He's the one I was talking to'. Similarly, French dominant French / English bilinguals say things like: 'He plays very well the guitar' which shows the same word order as the French: '*Il joue très bien la guitare*'.

Interference is one indication of language *dominance*. In those cases where the bilingual is not absolutely *balanced*, one language is said to be dominant. However, it follows from our discussion above about domains of interest and experience that it is not necessarily the same language that is always dominant. William, a French / English bilingual, went to school in France but to a cadet camp in England. When he wanted to talk about his school-life in English or army-life in French, he found that the relevant vocabulary and concepts were not always available. It is worth noting, though, that this is not necessarily a static situation; if William had to talk with a number of Frenchmen about his army-life he would almost certainly develop the necessary vocabulary, usually by simply assimilating that of his interlocutors.

The dominance of one language should not be thought of as in any way unhealthy or unusual. As we have seen, people who speak only one language have areas in which they are especially skilled (for example, skin diving, knitting, pigeon-fancying) and areas of complete ignorance. So do bilinguals. The problem is that people do not judge bilinguals by the standards they use to judge monolinguals: they judge them with reference to an impossible ideal, the 'native speaker' who supposedly speaks *all* possible varieties of his language, who can, *linguistically speaking*, do everything in all domains and on all topics in his language. If we look at the people we meet in the course of a single day, we see that we are requiring far more of the bilingual in both his languages than we would dream of expecting of a monolingual in one. Questions of specialised domains apart, we have to admit that our fellow native speakers differ amongst themselves in linguistic ability. Our next-door neighbour is well known for the marvellous way he has of telling stories and dramatising little anecdotes, but he can hardly write enough to cover the back of a postcard. Taciturn Uncle George, on the other hand, is an exquisite and entertaining letter-writer.

One further manifestation of dominance is the bilingual's *preference* for one of his languages. If you leave the choice of language to a bilingual and ask him to talk about a number of topics, a clear preference is soon discernible. However, it also needs to be noted that the idea that one is better in one language than another is sometimes completely subjective. This means that to an observer the bilingual's performance in each language may well be equally good. While the bilingual who feels that his weaker language is something of a strait-jacket may change to his preferred language only to find things are just as difficult.

Amongst the many variants of bilingualism one important one is known as *receptive bilingualism*. This means that the individual concerned understands the language, but cannot, will not or does not speak it. It is important both because it is very common and because outsiders often regard it as a 'refusal to speak' and consequently as a further demonstration that bilingualism does not work.

There are a number of causes of receptive bilingualism. The most important one is language shift, that is, situations where a group is changing from using one language to using another. Immigrant groups in the USA have provided some of the best-studied examples of language shift and of the receptive bilingualism which it gave rise to:

> Instead of a full competence, the children acquired only a partial competence. Writing fell away first, then reading. The effort required to impose these skills became too great for the parents. Similarly, the children succeeded in limiting the sphere within which Norwegian was spoken. They spoke it only to one or a few older members of the family, usually a grandparent, while they spoke English to all others. If their position was exceptionally strong, they succeeded in evading the speaking entirely, even to their parents. This bilingual situation was highly typical, with parents speaking Norwegian and children answering in English. Eventually the parents might also succumb to the pressure exerted by this uncomfortable situation and go over to English themselves.   (Haugen, 1969)

In a situation where language shift is taking place, parents end up losing their facility in the spoken language, in this case Norwegian. Renewed contact with native speakers would soon reactivate their ability to speak the language, but for their children the situation is different. Although they are able to understand the language and perhaps to read it, they cannot use it for the purposes of expression: they are in a state of receptive bilingualism.

If receptive bilingualism only occurred as a result of language shift it would not really concern us here, since it would be a social characteristic of immigrant populations. But there are other causes that are nearer to our present interests. The most important of these is a bilingual pattern where the parents use one language with one another and a different language with the children. In such circumstances, the children understand perfectly what the parents are saying but they never speak it themselves or speak it so seldom that they are regarded as unable to speak the language. Jan and Kasimir, who are English / Polish bilinguals, spoke English with their parents, but their parents continued to speak Polish to one another. As a result Jan and Kasimir were receptive bilinguals, who had no problems in understanding Polish but did not speak it. This is an extremely common pattern in bilingual families and a perfectly sound arrangement. Outsiders might criticise it, though, because the children 'don't speak the language', but one might just as well emphasise the positive aspects and say that the children do understand the language – and that the family as a whole has adopted an efficient system of communication.

Moreover, in such cases, if the parents suddenly decide to move back 'home', the children will usually develop their speaking ability in that language quickly and with little difficulty. This is obviously an important point to be borne in mind by parents who are likely to return to their country of origin after a number of years (at the end of a contract, for example, or to retire) or whose children are likely to return to that country for educational purposes or family visits.

A further important variant of receptive bilingualism involves one of the parents understanding but not speaking the language used between the other parent and the children. In the Riley family, for example, where the mother always communicates with the children in Swedish, while the father communicates with them in English, the father understands everything that is said in Swedish but never speaks a word of that language (on the rare occasions when he has tried, the children have rolled around on the floor laughing). Receptive bilingualism of this kind is vital to many patterns of successful bilingualism. Imagine what would happen in a situation where the parents spoke different languages to the children and where one or both of them could not understand the other's language. At the very least, there would have to be endless, tiresome translations and relaying of messages, and at the worst a real breakdown in communication. In fact, what usually happens in such circumstances is either that the 'odd man out' quickly develops receptive bilingualism or that the family becomes to all intents and purposes monolingual. This was the case of Nancy, an American woman married to a Frenchman who did not speak English. When their first son was born, Nancy spoke to him in English, but as soon as he became old enough to have a 'conversation' with his parents things got out of hand, since the exchange got bogged down in the father's incessant requests for explanations and translations. The family became monolingual French, at least for a time. Four years later, they had a second child, a girl, and the mother again tried to bring her up bilingually. By this time the father had picked up a certain amount of English and so things went much better: the trouble was that now it was the elder child, not the father, who constantly interrupted any English conversation, asking what it was about. Fortunately, as a result of extended stays in the USA, the son learnt enough English for him too to understand what was being said between mother and daughter and so the family has become to some extent bilingual. This case-history exemplifies the important point that neither the individual's bilingualism nor the pattern of bilingualism established within the family is static, fixed once and for all; many families shift from one arrangement to another as circumstances change. This, however, seems to be the general rule: *where one of the parents does not understand one of the languages, attempts to maintain bilingualism in the family are most likely to fail.* There may be exceptions of course, but we have come across so many examples of this happening that we feel justified in regarding it as almost inevitable.

A variation of receptive bilingualism is *asymmetrical bilingualism*, the ability to speak a language better than you understand it. In this respect, Beardsmore quotes the example of a French student of English going to the north of England for a holiday and finding that though people can understand him, he can't understand them – at least, not to start with. Parents should be aware that this can happen to children quite easily, and that it is not serious, since it is usually short-lived. It is not difficult to understand how asymmetrical bilingualism can occur. Take, for example, the cases of Ingrid and Matthias, sister and brother French / German bilinguals, who have learnt their German from their father, in France. Despite occasional trips to Germany, they simply are not exposed to the quantity or range of accents, voices or speaking styles to be found in Germany. They understand their father's German perfectly, but can be thrown by another German speaker who does not have exactly the same characteristics, because of age perhaps, or because he comes from a different part of the country. Once again, though, it is important to underline the point that monolinguals can have exactly the same sort of problem. Philip Riley's father, who was English, never learnt to understand Americans speaking, even after the advent of television, and anyone who has made a sudden move from, say, southern England to Scotland will need a period of adaptation. One feels for the sixteen-year-old French / English bilingual on holiday in Halifax, Yorkshire, who, when congratulated on her English because she 'didn't have an accent' replied: 'No – but *you* do!'

3.2   Compound and co-ordinate bilinguals

Perhaps we should state at the outset that this distinction is no longer a fashionable one. Specialists in bilingualism regard it as, at best, a drastic over-simplification. We have two main reasons for referring to it here, though. The first is that, in its time, it was very influential indeed and many books, articles and encyclopaedias still use these terms. The second, and more important, reason is that these concepts were developed to account for some of the most important characteristics of bilingualism. They ask the right questions, as it were, even if the answers are wrong.

The distinction between compound and co-ordinate bilinguals was made originally to account for differences in cognitive organisation in bilingual individuals. Such differences are usually associated with the context in which their bilingualism has been acquired, although there is no necessary one-to-one relationship between the two. The hypothesis was developed by Ervin and Osgood (1954) but was based on a suggestion by Weinreich (1953).

Weinreich was mainly concerned with the descriptive problems arising in situations where language systems were in contact. In the section of his book entitled 'The nature of the sign in language contact', he made a distinction between bilingualism of the co-ordinative type, bilingualism of a compound type and bilingualism of a subordinative type.

  i) *The co-ordinative type of bilingualism* applies to individuals who have two functionally independent systems.
 ii) *The compound type of bilingualism* applies to individuals who have two linguistic signs.
iii) *The subordinative type of bilingualism* applies to individuals who are dominant in one language. They have two linguistic signs but only one unit of meaning, which is that of the dominant language.

Perhaps it might help to clarify these three distinctions (at the risk of even further over-simplification, though) if we say that (i) applies to two completely separate systems both of meaning and expression, (ii) applies when there is only one system of meaning but two equal but separate systems of expression, and (iii) applies when there is one system of meaning, one dominant system of expression and one subordinate system of expression.

Ervin and Osgood were psychologists who were interested in the cognitive organisation of bilinguals, and in particular the cognitive representation of semantic units in bilingual individuals. They modified Weinreich's scheme and called type (i) bilinguals 'co-ordinate bilinguals' and types (ii) and (iii) 'compound bilinguals'. This hypothesis was attractive, since it allowed them to make hypotheses about how people brought up in a particular kind of environment would behave: a child brought up in a bilingual home where two different languages were used in the same environment by the same people would be more 'compound' than a child brought up with one language at home and one outside. In the first case, both languages would be acquired in the same context; in the second, the language would be acquired in two separate contexts.

A great deal of ink and effort went into devising increasingly sophisticated techniques for testing whether people were 'co-ordinate' or 'compound'. Unfortunately (for the hypothesis, that is) the vast majority of those tested turned out to be somewhere in between the two: 'typical' co-ordinate behaviour and 'typical' compound behaviour hardly ever existed.

In 1970, Diller condemned the distinction as a 'conceptual artifact' on the grounds that the three categories proposed by Weinreich had been misconstrued and that Weinreich did not want to restrict his distinction to word-meaning but wished to see it applied to other levels of language such as grammar and sound-structure. This was an important point, since one of the characteristics of the testing techniques used by psychologists was that they relied almost exclusively on word lists and 'translation equivalents', failing thereby to take grammar and phonology into account.

Moreover, even at word level, it is easy to see that the notion of the absolute independence of the two languages (co-ordinate) or the complete fusion (compound) is highly artificial. In most pairs of languages there are words which have identical meanings, and in theory this should prevent 'typical co-ordinates' from even existing. For example, as far as we know, an English 'python' is very much like a French *python*. Other words have similar, but not identical ranges of meaning like French *table* and English 'table'. And finally there are those words which have little in common, even though they appear to be equivalent. A good example is the pair 'comfortable' and *confortable* (French for 'comfortable, snug, cosy', according to Harrap's *New Shorter French and English Dictionary*). Compare these sentences: 'He is comfortable in hospital' and '*Il a une situation confortable*' ('He has a secure job and no money problems'). So even if we do restrict our attention to word level, it is clear that a bilingual *cannot* be totally co-ordinate or totally compound.

In 1972 Lambert produced a new definition which introduces the criterion of the *age* at which the second language was introduced. Compound bilinguals were defined as:

> those brought up in a throughly bilingual home environment from infancy on, while co-ordinates were those who learned the second language at some time after infancy, usually after ten years of age and usually in a setting other than the family.

Without recognising it, this is a major modification of the original distinction. By redefining the distinction in this way, Lambert places the issue of how we classify different types of bilingual within the framework of the debate about the age at which the 'second' language should be introduced (see *Age* in Part III).

One final point which further throws the usefulness and validity of the compound / co-ordinate distinction into question is that bilingual subjects *change* over time. A 'co-ordinate' bilingual may become a 'compound' one and vice versa, depending on what they do and how they use their two languages. As Macnamara (1970) states:

> The manner in which a person has learned his languages is unlikely to fix his semantic systems for life.

For example, a Frenchwoman who has been living in England for over ten years and uses French every day at home with her English husband in a completely English environment is likely to exhibit a more compound type of behaviour on vocabulary tests now than at the time of her arrival.

3.3 Age of acquisition

It is convenient to distinguish between at least four ages at which individuals become bilingual. These are: infancy, childhood, adolescence and adulthood.

Infant bilingualism

This term shocks purists, as 'infant' originally meant 'unable to speak'. But perhaps its use is unintentionally precise, as it underlines the fact that the baby in question goes directly from not speaking at all to speaking two languages.

That is, cases of infant bilingualism necessarily involve the *simultaneous acquisition* of both languages. Amongst the families we observed and interviewed for this book, this was one of the most common and successful types of bilingualism. Let us look at a typical example.

Philip was born in England. His mother is French and his father is English. He has had regular contacts with the French side of his family and has spent holidays in France. When he started reading at school he also started looking through and deciphering French books at home and he became 'biliterate'. At the age of six he had the opportunity to spend several months in France and so went to a French primary school, where he had no difficulty. When asked his feelings about knowing two languages, he says it is 'normal', but regrets that he hasn't learnt German as well – but he is taking steps in that direction by playing with his German / French bilingual cousin!

In some cases of infant bilingualism, where the parents speak one language at home and the child stays at home all day with his mother, the outside language will be learned by the child only in a receptive way (see section 3.1 above). He goes to the shops with his mother, he listens to the radio, watches television, hears his parents talking with visitors and friends, and so on, but does not usually feel the need to use the outside language *actively* until he makes friends with the neighbours' children or goes to a playgroup or nursery school. This is all perfectly natural – just another instance of the child not using a language until and unless he *needs* to. The important thing is for parents not to panic and start imagining that because Jean-Marc has not started speaking English at, say, three years of age, he will never do so. He will do so when he needs to, that is, when he starts meeting English-speaking adults and children. We should look at the child's social life before we start worrying about his language acquisition.

In very general statistical terms, bilingual infants and children start speaking slightly later than monolinguals, but they still remain well within the degrees of variation for monolingual children. In other words, they start speaking at an age that is perfectly acceptable in a monolingual child. In fact the age difference between girls and boys (girls start speaking, on average, several weeks before boys) is bigger than the difference between monolinguals and bilinguals. Other causes of variation that need to be kept in mind include the child's position in the family: first-born children usually start speaking earlier than subsequent children because they do not have to share their parents' attention. Lastly, there is individual variation, which can be considerable. The average range is from eight to fifteen months. It is also perfectly ordinary to have such differences occurring between children in the same family: Margaret, a first-born girl, was producing expressions like: 'There it is!' before her seventh month, whilst her little brother was well over three years old before he managed anything more than his sister's name and the word 'No!'. He then caught up with her.

Child bilingualism

Child bilingualism seems to assume the *successive acquisition* of two languages, but the distinction between simultaneous and sequential acquisition is not always clear. In particular, McLaughlin (1978) proposed that acquisition of more than one language up to age three should be considered simultaneous but, as pointed out by Romaine (1999), it seems to be an arbitrary criterion. Since the most common cause of successive acquisition is the family's moving to another country, it often corresponds to a difficult period of adaptation in the child's life and obviously this includes learning the language. None the less, experience has shown time and time again that children in this situation will learn a second language with amazing rapidity *if they are exposed to it*. Obviously, the degree of help the child gets from teachers and classmates will be important, but it is difficult to generalise about such things (see *School* in Part III). By and large, in the cases we have examined, parents said they were surprised and relieved to see how smoothly their children made the transition. Two Portuguese children (five-and-a-half and three-and-a-half) starting at a French nursery school in September were said to be 'linguistically indistinguishable from the other children within five months' and this is not an exceptional case.

The astonishing facility with which young children learn a second language is only paralleled by the speed at which they can forget one. Again, the crucial factors are use and need. If a language no longer serves the child's communicative needs he will not use it and if he doesn't use it he will forget it, quickly and completely.

Antoine, the first child of an Austrian / French couple living in Brazil, was brought up speaking Portuguese as his first language. At the age of three-and-a-half he moved 'back' to France with his parents. In less than ten months he had forgotten all his Portuguese except one word, but his French, which until then had been only receptive, was almost 'native' (see Case Study 5).

Since families are not static entities, it is quite possible to find that children in the same family may become bilingual in different ways. For example, children moving to a new country with their parents will, as we have seen, set about the successive acquisition of the second language. On the other hand, small brothers and sisters born once the family has settled down there will, if the relevant pattern is established, acquire the two languages simultaneously.

Families that move frequently from one country to another may accumulate and shed languages in a way that seems almost casual to the outside observer. A British Council officer who had worked in Europe, the Middle East, South America and Scandinavia remarked that his elder children had 'learnt six languages and forgotten five of them'. Since they had always kept up their English, though, he felt there was no harm done.

Under certain circumstances, however, the accumulated languages may all be maintained. The best example of this that we know of at first hand is a four-year-old Indian child who speaks five languages (though, as his mother pointed out, 'he finds it rather hard to be polite in English'). In the Riley family, which is trilingual, the pattern developed as follows: the mother and father always communicated in English, but the mother began speaking Swedish to their first child who was born in Finland. This also helped the father to learn Swedish, though he continued to speak English with his wife and with the new baby. The second child was born in Malta, into a family which was already bilingual. Brother and sister usually speak to one another in English. A move to France followed. The two children learnt French at school extremely rapidly and with no noticeable problems, an example of the successive acquisition of a third language. A third child was born in France: she has learnt English and Swedish at home and French outside, this being, therefore, an example of the simultaneous acquisition of three languages. By five, her linguistic level was roughly the same in all three languages. By the end of her French secondary schooling, French had certainly become dominant. However, she then spent four years in the UK and is now working for an international company where she uses both French and English on a regular basis. Her case illustrates that dominance in childhood can in no way determine patterns of dominance as an adult.

Later bilingualism

Adolescent bilingualism is a term used to refer to people who have become bilingual *after puberty*. Adult bilingualism is used for people who become bilingual after their teens. Whereas infant and child bilingualism are usually associated with a native or native-like pronunciation, later bilingualism is often associated with a non-native accent. (See Chapter 4.)

3.4 Sharing two cultures

Culture, the 'way of life' of the society in which we grow up, influences our habits, our customs, the way we dress and eat, our beliefs and values, our ideas and feelings, our notions of politeness and beauty. Most aspects of culture are assimilated unconsciously, simply by living in a particular society, and most of them are directly related to language in some way. There is a universal tendency to confuse one's own cultural habits with the immutable laws of nature and for this reason we only actually become aware of them when we are confronted with people from other walks of life or other countries. Moreover, when we do become aware of them, we often react with a deep sense of shock. Our world can be turned upside down when we learn that 'they' eat snails, mint sauce or sheeps' eyes.

Biculturalism refers to the co-existence of two cultures in the same individual. Bilingualism and biculturalism do not necessarily coincide; as we saw earlier, in countries where several languages co-exist, and in particular where there is a lingua franca used for educational and administrative purposes, most people are bilingual but they belong to one predominant culture. On the other hand, many monolinguals are bicultural, such as the growing number of business people, academics and entertainers who are 'equally at home' in Britain or the USA. So, too, are those Irish, Scots and Welsh people who, despite having English as their sole language, maintain a cultural identity which they do not share with the English (for example, in terms of institutions such as the legal or educational systems, and in their tastes and customs).

Because each individual only has one life and one identity, the notion that the same person can be entirely German in Germany with Germans and entirely French in France with French people is somewhat unrealistic. On the whole, people whose lives are shared between two communities exhibit various combinations of two distinct cultures. They may feel at ease in both cultures, behave perfectly appropriately in both communities, but their double allegiance will naturally crop up here and there. Only in cases of tension between the two communities will this be a problem, and not always then. Only spies really need to hide from others the meaningful references which make up the fabric of their lives. To 'give yourself away' is communicative generosity, not bad manners of some kind and we can only understand people to the extent that we know them. We reveal something about ourselves with our every utterance and for the bilingual it may well be something about his 'other' culture. Take, for example, the Englishman who has been living in France for over ten years but who is still capable of evoking the disruption caused by the arrival of a baby in the following terms: 'Social life, over! Lying in on Sunday morning, finished! A quick one down the pub every fortnight – if you're lucky!'

When the individual is suddenly plunged into a new culture, he or she often undergoes what is generally known as 'culture shock'. The symptoms of this state have been described as follows:

> Culture shock might be called an occupational disease of people who have been suddenly transported abroad ... [it] is precipitated by the anxiety that

results from losing all our familiar signs and symbols of social intercourse . . . a series of props have been knocked from under you, followed by a feeling of frustration and anxiety. People react to the frustration in much the same way. First they reject the environment which causes the discomfort.   (Kalervo Oberg, 1972, quoted in Casse, 1984)

One's chances of learning a language in a state of culture shock are very slight, as the language (and the people who speak it) forms a major part of the environment which is rejected. But culture shock is by no means limited to those who do not yet speak the language or to the socially disadvantaged. A recent European survey of the attitudes of university students who spend a period of residence abroad as part of their degree shows that highly proficient individuals can resent the host country as a result of cultural differences (Coleman,1996). Paradoxically, it is often the fact that such students do speak the language of the host country that makes their lives difficult. If you make grammatical mistakes or use the wrong words, people think you *speak* badly, but if you make cultural mistakes, they think you *behave* badly.

Although children can suffer from culture shock as badly as any adult, in our experience (and with reference only to the kind of middle-class family we have been discussing) it is usually less traumatic and shorter lived. They are protected by their parents, they do not have their parents' responsibilities and they are remarkably resilient and adaptable. The rapidity with which they learn the language and integrate into the host society, simply by going to the local school, for example, means that usually they feel quite at home well before their parents. It is certainly not unknown for the children to play a major role in getting their own parents to understand and accept the ways of the host society. Of course, where one of the parents is actually a citizen of the 'new' country – when a Czech / French couple moves 'back' to France, for instance – such problems are considerably reduced. This is in itself a major argument for bringing children up bilingually, though of course it might not be sufficient to do away with all the difficulties caused by being uprooted.

It is also worth noting that where the parents 'overadjust' in their desire to be accepted by the new community, where they abandon their original culture and language, it is sometimes seen as a kind of 'treason' by the children. It is not uncommon for a child to insist on learning his parents' language; indeed, in our experience most children after the age of puberty will want to do so. They will not all do so to the same degree, of course. Dominique, son of a French father and an English mother, was brought up speaking only French. At the age of thirteen he began to take an interest in English, England and the English. Soon he was insisting that his mother speak English with him. He now no longer lives at home, but continues to speak English with her; she found it extremely difficult to change such long-standing habits, but was willing to try and very happy with the results. Dominique now speaks a fluent, almost accent-free English and is majoring in that language at a university in France. A further example is that of Barbara, a second-generation American child in an Italian immigrant family who had been brought up to speak only English: she is now in Italy, learning the language and making a particular study of the dialect spoken in the region her family originally came from.

Children from bilingual families will be aware that, somehow, they are expected to identify with the behaviour of two different cultures. Where the situation does not actually involve antipathy between the two cultures, this is unlikely to disturb them. For example, Philip, aged six, is staying in France with his French mother. He watches her prepare spinach, which he loves, for lunch. After a long silence, he declares: 'Too bad if little French children don't like spinach; this lunchtime I'm English'.

There are a number of studies that show that adolescents from mixed parentage can be truly bicultural instead of rejecting one of the cultures. Significantly, all these studies (Aellen and Lambert, 1969; Peal and Lambert, 1962; Lambert and Tucker, 1972) were conducted in Canada on English / French bilinguals whose parents, if not always bicultural themselves, were very favourably disposed to their children becoming so. Lambert writes:

> Rather than cultural conflicts we find well-adjusted young people with broad perspectives who are comfortable in the role of representing both of their cultural backgrounds. We also have here an illustration of the *additive* form of biculturalism: the boys studied were caught in the flow of two cultural streams and were apparently happy to be part of both streams.
>
> (cited in Hornby, 1977)

It is not just chance that both the languages and cultures here were high status, but we feel that for culture just as for language, it is very easy to create problems where there are none. In a great majority of cases, adjusting to a new cultural world coincides for the child with a time when he would have had to adjust to a new culture (or sub-culture) in his own country or community. Individuals are not 'monocultural': they belong to different groups at different times and periods in their lives, and for each of these groups there are accepted rules of behaviour and ways of talking.

You do not behave and talk in your football club in the same way as you do with your colleagues at work or your family at home. So-called 'monocultural' couples must be something of a rarity. In most cases, the two partners have to adjust to each other's cultural background. For instance, Edith Harding-Esch's mother came from a 'petit bourgeois' Catholic background while her father came from a Protestant farming family. True, the grandparents did not cook or dress or react in the same way, but the children all survived without traumas and after some thirty-odd years of life in common the parents had built something like a family culture of their own. This is certainly no exception.

In this chapter we have looked at how patterns of use and cultural context may influence a child's type of bilingualism. We are now going to move on in Chapter 4 to discuss the child's language development and the ways in which bilinguals can exploit their command of two languages as an extra resource for communication.

....

CHAPTER FOUR

The development of the bilingual child

SIMULTANEOUS ACQUISITION

Most of what we know about the simultaneous acquisition of two lan-guages by children is based on case studies or reports produced by parents-cum-linguists observing their own children. As often as not, these studies take the form of a 'linguistic diary' recording a child's development during all or part of her early childhood.

From a strictly scientific point of view, such a procedure has an obvious disadvantage, namely, that the results cannot really be regarded as objective or generalisable, since the parents, just because they are parents, may distort the results. None the less, improvements in record-ing techniques, and in particular the use of video and sound recordings, make such data not only increasingly reliable for research (Deuchar and Quay, 2000; Vihman, 1999) but extremely useful to would-be bilingual families, since they show that it has been done before, and done success-fully.

By 'successful', we mean here that *all* the children who have been studied in this way have grown up to be perfectly 'normal', none of them having exhibited any sign of being disturbed by their experience. Moreover, these children, while usually dominant in one of their lan-guages at the time their case was reported, were none the less able to use their other languages when circumstances required. This phenomenon has been observed frequently, although for the parents concerned there will, naturally enough, always be a sense of wonder when it happens. An example is given in Case Study 3: a monolingual German grandmother came to stay with her daughter, French son-in-law and grandson. The grandson, aged three, had up to that point said very little in German, but when he realised that Grandmother could not understand his French he launched into fluent, acceptable German.

We make this point here to underline the fact that children, in linguistic as in other matters, are by no means completely predictable. In the end, as discussed by De Houwer (1999), much of the immediate language environment in which the child acquires his languages and which determines – amongst other things – the frequency with which parents use a particular language to the child, is influenced by the parents' attitudes and beliefs. So the 'categories' of childhood bilinguals mentioned below and in our own case studies should be taken with a pinch of salt. The main use of such categories is that it provides a basis of comparison that helps individual families describe and identify their own situation. But do not be surprised if you do not find a family, here or in the case studies, which corresponds exactly to your circumstances, as an almost infinite number of variations are possible. A number of typologies have been proposed in the past ten years and each of them has advantages related to the specific interest of their authors. For example, Döpke's (1992) typology is based on interactional principles and the patterns of exposure that can be predicted from the way the 'one parent one language principle' is applied in different environments. The recent categorisation proposed by Yamamoto (2001) stresses the fact that 'interlingual families' are a context in which children are only potentially bilingual. It is particularly relevant to the Japanese context where the constructs 'native language' and 'community language' appear to be less problematic than in Europe. Our typology was used as a basis by Romaine (1995 [2nd ed.]), and recently Tokuhama-Espinosa (2001) developed it to include multilingual children. The latter is also nearest to us in spirit because of the educational orientation and of the author's overt acceptance of the complex dynamics of families: parents cannot always control the application of the strategy they have decided upon as if the family members were experimental subjects but often 'bumble their way into being a truly multilingual (or bilingual) household' (p. 57).

4.1   Types of bilingual families

The following five main types of bilingual families have been described in the technical literature on bilingualism. Each type has its own characteristics, described below. The studies mentioned are entered under the author's name in the reference section at the end of the book.

1 Parents   The parents have different native languages: each parent has some degree of competence in the other's language.

   Community   The language of one of the parents is the dominant language of the community.

   Strategy   The parents each speak their own language to the child from birth.

Studies include:

Author's name	Mother's language	Father's language	Community language
Ronjat	German	French	French
Leopold	German	US English	US English
Raffler-Engel	Italian	US English	Italian
Taeschner	German	Italian	Italian
Arnberg	English: various dialects	Swedish	Swedish
Tokuhama-Espinosa	Spanish-French	French-Spanish	French + German

Case Studies 1, 3, 7 and 11 in Part II fall into this category.

2 Parents   The parents have different native languages.

   Community   The language of one of the parents is the dominant language of the community.

   Strategy   Both parents speak the non-dominant language to the child, who is only fully exposed to the dominant language when outside the home and in particular when he or she starts nursery school.

Studies include:

Author's name	Mother's language	Father's language	Community language
Fantini	Sth Am. Spanish	US English	US English
Zierer	Spanish	German	Peruvian Spanish
Deuchar	UK English	Spanish	UK English
Vihman	US English	Estonian	US English

This is the case of E. Harding-Esch's family.

3 Parents   The parents share the same native language.

   Community   The dominant language is not that of the parents.

   Strategy   The parents speak their own language to the child.

Studies include:

Author's name	Parents' language	Community language
Haugen	Norwegian	US English
Bubenik	Czech	Canadian English
Oksaar	Estonian	Swedish followed by German
Ruke-Dravina	Latvian	Swedish

Case Studies 2, 8, 15 and 16 in Part II fall into this category.

4   Parents   The parents have different native languages.
    Community   The dominant language is different from either of the parents' languages.
    Strategy   The parents each speak their own language to the child from birth.

Studies include:

Author's name	Mother's language	Father's language	Community language
Elwert	Br. English	German	Italian

Case Study 5 in Part II falls into this category. It is also the case of P. Riley's family.

5   Parents   The parents share the same native language.
    Community   The dominant language is the same as that of the parents.
    Strategy   One of the parents always addresses the child in a language which is not his or her native language.

Studies include:

Author's name	Parents' language	Second language chosen	Community language
Past	US English	Spanish	US English
Dimitrijević	Serbian	English	Serbian
Saunders	Aust. English	German	Aust. English

What do published case studies tell us?

In summarising the evidence contained in published studies, McLaughlin (1978) writes (the italics are ours):

> In short, it seems that *the language acquisition process is the same in its basic features and in its developmental sequence for the bilingual child and the monolingual child.* The bilingual child has the *additional task of distinguishing the two language systems,* but there is no evidence that this requires special language processing devices.

In other words, the bilingual child learns two languages in the same way and in the same order as the monolingual child learns one, with the obvious difference that the bilingual child has to learn to distinguish between the two. Moreover, the mechanisms involved in the differentiation of the two languages by a bilingual are not different in nature from those used by monolinguals to make distinctions within their one linguistic system. Thus, bilingualism does not require any special mental processes, but only an extension and refinement of those common to all language speakers.

Let us now look in more detail at the two main points that are made, namely, that both monolinguals and bilinguals develop in the same way and that the bilingual child has to learn to distinguish between the two languages.

4.2   Similarities in development between bilinguals and monolinguals

In general terms, the rate and pattern of language development are the same for monolingual and bilingual children. True, there is a widespread impression amongst the parents of many bilingual children that their children start speaking later than monolingual children. On the other hand, in a study in which mothers were asked to note their child's 'first word', bilinguals averaged 11.2 months as against the monolinguals' average of 12 months (Doyle et al., 1978). Such results are not particularly reliable, however, as any proud parent knows: just when does that lip-smacking gurgle begin to count as a real word? The difference in these averages could equally be a reflection of the parents' linguistic strictness. The impression of lateness reported so often by the parents we interviewed might just be a result of impatience or anxiety. If anything, it is the closeness of the two averages which is significant.

More reliable is the observation that both monolinguals and bilinguals start by producing words with sounds that are simpler to articulate ('p', 'b', 'd', 'f', 'm', 'n') leaving the more difficult sounds such as 'ch' and 'j' (as in 'jump') till later, as well as the groups of consonants ('fr', 'st') and the diphthongs. Both groups of children also extend the meanings of words to things which appear to them to be the same. Again, both mono- and bilinguals will slowly increase the length of their utterances, and start by using simple constructions before embarking on complex ones like relative clauses.

To put it succinctly, the similarities between bilingual and monolingual children are far more striking than the differences.

4.3   Separating the two languages

There are two schools of thought regarding the separation of their two languages by bilingual children. There are those who think they go through an initial mixed stage and combine the two languages into one unified system and there are those who believe that they keep both languages separate from the moment they start talking.

It is worth noting that this question does not seem to worry bilingual children unduly. However, the issue is a very important one for linguists and psychologists, if only because it prevents them from labelling what the children produce with any degree of certainty. In particular, one simply cannot talk about the *interference* of one language with another if there is no evidence that there are two separate systems. For example, if a three-year-old English / Swedish child says: '*Det är en* snowman' it can be taken as clear evidence that *either* the child produces mixed utterances which reflect her inability to separate the two languages *or* that the child has two distinct systems, since the correct word order is preserved (there are no unnecessary words, for example, '*Det är en* a snowman') and, most important of all, the accentuation and pronunciation is correct: '*det är en*' is pronounced with a Swedish accent, 'snowman' with an English accent. The Swedish part of the utterance follows the rules of Swedish, the English part follows the rules of English. The fact that the utterance itself is mixed can be explained in a number of other ways, the most likely being that the child hears such mixed utterances in its environment. Certainly, such utterances are said to be typical of children who are themselves exposed to mixed utterances.

This, it must be admitted, is a pretty unsatisfactory state of affairs for the psycholinguist, but gradually, researchers get to understand more and more. For example, research in experimental phonetics on French / English primary bilinguals has shown that there are subtle interactions between the sound systems of their languages (Watson 2002). In other words, bilinguals are different from monolinguals and do not process their two languages as if they were two separate systems. But however important such findings concerning the interdependence of the two languages in the brain is for theoreticians, the important point to remember for parents is that it can only be demonstrated through complex statistical analysis. In other words, these are differences that cannot be detected in the course of day-to-day social interaction with the children. So, in practice, parents should not forget the following points:

- Some children never mix, or only very rarely.
- Most children mix very early on and then gradually get things sorted out.
- 'Mixing' is part of the process of getting things sorted out.

This third point is an important one for parents, who naturally tend to interpret a mixed utterance as evidence of confusion when in fact the child is getting on with the task of building up two sets of patterns by making more and more subtle contrasts: in our example, the separate rules that have been applied to the Swedish part of the utterance and the English part are quite complex grammatically. Moreover, the overall structure of the utterance is correct for *both* Swedish and English, whereas the mixing ('snowman' for *snö-gubbe*) is a very simple one indeed.

The most convincing description of how bilingual children develop remains Volterra and Taeschner's three-main-phase model (1978). It can be briefly summarised as follows.

Phase 1

During the first phase, the child has one lexical system ('vocabulary') which includes words from both languages *but* where pairs of words have not yet been matched up. The child operates on a *one-word-for-one-concept principle*: either only one of the words in the pair is used or the two words are used with different meanings. This second possibility is illustrated by the case of a little Italian / German girl who used to use *la* to refer to things which were not visible and *da* for things she could see. Another example is that of the Swedish / English child who used *stol* (chair) for her (high-) chair and 'chair' for all other chairs.

The words used at this stage are sometimes constructed from the two languages, thus producing *blends* or *compounds* which tend to frighten parents. Emma, an English / French bilingual produced the following example of a blend over a period of several months: 'tati', a blend of 'thank you' and *merci*. Other examples of blends, cited by Grosjean (1982), include 'shot' (*chaud* and 'hot'), 'pinichon' ('pickle' and *cornichon*) and 'assit' (*assis* and 'sit'). A compound is one word made up of a pair of corresponding words from the two languages. Leopold's daughter would say '*bitte*-please' (Leopold, 1954) and Grosjean reports '*lune*-moon' and even '*pour*-for'. Emily, a Swedish / English 16-month-old, regularly said '*tack*-thank you', '*ärter*-peas' and so on. A considerable amount of research has recently been carried out on mixed two-word utterances in early bilinguals acquiring different pairs of languages. They indicate that the content words (or 'vocabulary') and the function words (or 'grammar') are used differently by the child in a characteristic way. Content words seem to match the language context and to belong to two separate developing systems whereas function words are 'context neutral' and seem to be available irrespective of language source in both language contexts (Deuchar and Vihman, 2002). In other words, what appears to be confusion to the parents is in reality the outcome of extremely complex and subtle processes making it possible for the child to respond to the complexities of the linguistic situation in a flexible way.

Very early on, the same phenomenon seems to apply to sounds: the child has one unified system made up of sounds from both languages. Leopold concludes his analysis of the development of his daughter Hildegard (English / German) with the observation that:

> Thus [she] had, by the end of the second year, a slightly wider experience with sounds than monolingual children: but they still belonged to a unified set of phonemes not differentiated by languages.

Informal observations reported to us by parents confirm this view: 'When our son started, he sounded the same in both languages. It was only as time passed he began to have two different accents.'

Phase 2

The child is now beginning to have two separate vocabularies, but applies the same rudimentary grammatical rules to both languages.

The picture is very complex at this point: some words are by now clearly differentiated, for instance 'horse' and *cheval* (Celce-Murcia, 1975) but when the words are similar but not identical (from the point of view of pronunciation usually) the child will often hesitate. For instance, Philip (English / French) would point at an orange and say *orange* in French with an exaggerated stress on the last syllable and then say 'orange' in English, with the stress on the first. At the same time, a child might continue to have a number of words for which she has no equivalent in the other language. Often, too, she will avoid a word in one of the languages if it is difficult to pronounce. Here is an example, where her father is trying to get Marguerite (German / French, 2 yrs 6 mths) to say the word *Knopf* ('button'):

> FATHER: *Knopf.*
> MARGUERITE: Nopf.
> FATHER: *Knopf.*
> MARGUERITE: Nopf.
> FATHER: *Knopf.*
> MARGUERITE: Bouton.

At this stage, too, children will frequently insert words from one language in a sentence in the other language. For example, Pierre (French / German, 2 yrs 6 mths): *Maman, Marguerite et Philip ils sont dans le* Baum. ('Mummy, Marguerite and Philip are in the tree.')

One of the clearest signs that the child is developing two separate vocabularies is that she is now beginning to be able to *translate* from one language to the other:

> EMMA: (English / French, 2 yrs 1 mth) Bye-bye doy. (i.e. 'dolly'.)
> MOTHER: *Qu'est-ce que dit maman?* ('What does Mummy say?')
> EMMA: *Auwar.* (i. e. '*au revoir.*') ('Good-bye.')

For the moment, the child seems to use only one set of grammatical rules, though of course this will only be obvious where the two languages have different rules. For example, the idea of *possession* in English and French is differentiated by word order, which results in exchanges like the following. Emma (2 yrs 2 mths) has just been talking with her English child-minder about 'Mummy car' (i.e. 'Mummy's car').

> MOTHER: *Qu'est-ce que tu vois là, Emma?* ('What do you see there, Emma?')
> EMMA: *Maman ature.* (i.e. '*maman voiture.*') ('Mummy car.')
> MOTHER: *Oui, c'est la voiture de maman.* ('Yes, it's Mummy's car.')
> EMMA: *Maman voiture.* ('Mummy car.')

Phase 3

The two languages are now differentiated as regards both vocabulary and grammar.

This is the stage where some children rigidly associate the languages with particular people. Hildegard, Leopold's daughter, asked her English-speaking mother: 'Mother, do all fathers speak German?' We would suggest that two related things are happening here: the first is that the child is beginning to map out her world socially – who speaks what language to whom. Here is an example: Katja (Swedish / English / French, 5 yrs) has just been collected from her French nursery school: 'Daddy, do my friends all speak English when they get home?'. Secondly, the child is probably attempting to reduce the effort involved in selecting the right words and structures. However, this tendency to label people according to their language decreases as the child becomes more confident in her use of the two languages.

Some children have a tendency to overgeneralise certain rules in order to help themselves keep the two languages separate. Philip (English / French, 6 yrs) has noticed that most adjectives in French go after the noun. He apparently wants *all* adjectives to go *before* the noun in English and *all* adjectives to be *after* the noun in French:

> GRANDFATHER: *Oui, c'est une belle maison.* ('Yes, it's a nice house.')
> PHILIP: *Non, c'est une maison belle en français.* ('No, it's a "house which is beautiful" in French.')

A few remarks are in order here:

i)   First, very little is actually known about the *process of separation* which bilingual children undergo. What we do know, though, is that they eventually get there and that mixed utterances decrease in number quickly.

ii) Secondly, the various phases described above can vary tremendously in length from child to child. *It is not possible to say at what age a child will reach a particular phase.* The phases are only convenient points on a continuum. Amongst the factors that we have mentioned as playing an important part in the child's development as regards separation of the two languages are:
     – Separation of context (and persons).
     – The quantity and quality of the interactions in each language.
     – The parents' attitude to mixing.

iii) Thirdly, interference and mixing is usually kept to a minimum in bilingual children if the two languages are kept in balance and if their domains of use are clearly separated (McLaughlin, 1978).

iv) Finally, 'dominance' is not static – it cannot be. When a bilingual family moves from one country to another, the pattern of linguistic input to the child may be entirely changed. A Spanish / German child brought up in Spain has got used to everything around her being in Spanish except what her father says; suddenly, after a move to Germany, everything is in German except what her mother says. In such circumstances, it is to be expected that the child will shift from dominance in Spanish to dominance in German. Indeed, in extreme cases, she may even seem to forget one language for a while.

This should be no cause for concern for the parents. For instance, until the age of three Marguerite was brought up in Germany by her German-speaking father and French-speaking mother and a German-speaking childminder. She then moved to France and was looked after by a French childminder. Within a week, she switched from playing with her dolls in German to playing in French. A few months later, when the family went back to Germany on a visit, she seemed to have forgotten German almost entirely. Her father continued to address her in German, but was not at home very much and did not spend much time with her.

At this point, her parents decided to send Marguerite to Germany whenever possible for brief holidays with her previous childminder. They also took on a German au pair. By about six months after the move, Marguerite's two languages were again developing in parallel.

Structural differences between the two languages may also make the child appear dominant in one language. If the same idea can be expressed by a simple grammatical rule in one language but requires a complex structure in a second language, the child will almost certainly learn the simpler rule first leading to a temporary imbalance. Mikeš (1967), for example, reports that two Hungarian / Serbo-Croatian children learnt to express the locative relation (roughly speaking, the 'whereabouts' of an object) earlier in Hungarian than in Serbo-Croatian. This was explained by the fact that in Hungarian location is marked by inflecting the noun, whereas in Serbo-Croatian there is not only inflection of the noun, but also a special locative preposition. Thus, for a time at least, the children appeared to be dominant in Hungarian because the same idea is more difficult to express in Serbo-Croatian.

When a child is temporarily dominant in one language for external reasons, as in the case of Marguerite, or for internal reasons, as in the example just given, the separation of the two languages can sometimes be delayed, because the stronger language influences the weaker one. This can happen at the levels of pronunciation or of grammar: Fantini quotes his son (4 yrs 6 mths) as saying: 'Watch me dress me', which is clearly modelled on the Spanish pronoun case

(Mirame vestirme). Again, Philip (6 yrs 1 mth) said: *J'ai fait la voiture tomber* ('I made the car fall') where he should have said: *J'ai fait tomber la voiture* ('I made fall the car').

   Such phenomena should not worry parents. They are the results of the child trying to express herself in her weaker language, and they will gradually disappear if the child is not cut off from contact with speakers of that language. However, it has to be emphasised that if the input in one language (that is, the occasions the child has to speak or hear it) is very much lower in one language than another, then that language will be correspondingly weaker and errors of this kind will take correspondingly longer to disappear.

4.4   Awareness of being a bilingual

When is a child aware that she is using two languages? And how can we make this sort of statement with confidence? Specialists disagree on both these issues. None the less, observation does show that from about three years old children do *use* their two or three languages in appropriate and consistent ways. For them, that is, language choice is no longer a problem. Another sign is that the child may translate for people who cannot understand:

> FATHER: Right, Kat, we're going to eat. Have you washed your hands?
> KATJA: (to her French friends) *Hé! On va manger. Il faut se laver les mains.*

(For more comment on *translating* see Part III.)

   It is about this time too, that children begin making comments on the fact that there are two languages. At first glance, this might seem to be incontrovertible evidence that they are aware of being bilingual themselves, but in fact the situation is not always so obvious. For example, it is not unusual for children to ask what language they are actually speaking, for example: 'What language am I talking now?' (Finn) and 'Daddy, am I talking to you in English?' (Katja). Another problem is that the child's notion of 'a language' simply does not coincide with the adult concept. In strictly sociolinguistic terms, the child's refusal to accept watertight compartments for her languages is often a far more accurate and realistic version of the facts than the adult's categories. This often manifests itself as an inability on the child's part to grasp the meaning of words like 'English', 'Spanish', 'French', 'German', 'Swedish' and so on. Not only are such terms too abstract but, given the child's experience, they are the wrong sort of abstraction. It is quite possible for children to use circumlocutions such as 'the way I speak to Mummy / Daddy / my friends / at school' until as late as the age of seven. Notice that these 'circumlocutions' are in fact far more accurate descriptions *from the child's point of view.*

Many children seem to go through a phase of 'checking' on their languages:

> KATJA: I speak like this to you and I speak, er, *på svenska* . . .
> FATHER: Swedish.
> KATJA: Swedish to Mummy and at school I speak *allemand*. (At her French nursery school, experimental German classes had just been introduced!)

To the outsider, this may sound a bit like showing off and there are occasions, no doubt, when it is precisely that. However, this behaviour is so common amongst small children who have no idea that being bilingual is 'special' for other people, that one is forced to look for other explanations. The most likely – again, we are in the realms of speculation – is that the child is affirming her identity: this is what I am like, this is who I am and what makes me tick.

It is usually clear when the child has no inkling of the fact that she is bilingual and when she has a clear perception of herself as a bilingual person. It is the period of transition which is difficult to pin down. When Katja started nursery school (3 yrs 1 mth) she became very cross because the French children wouldn't sing 'London bridge is falling down' with her. By the time she was five-and-a-half she insisted on a strict observation of all linguistic demarcation lines. The three- to five-year-old period is a crucial one for the social development of any child but the example illustrates the fact that for bilingual children it is accompanied by an extra-linguistic dimension which seems to be a source of fascination and pleasure: one of Katja's favourite 'chores' was to find BBC Radio 4 on the radio for her father.

To conclude this section, then, we can say that bilingual children do not differ from monolinguals as far as their language development is concerned, but naturally they do make distinctions that are hardly likely to be made by monolinguals because their world is different. This can lead to the occasional remark which is most entertaining for the parents, but baffling for outsiders. For example, Philip (3 yrs 1 mth) has just crossed over from England to France with his mother. They stop *en route* at a village shop to buy some biscuits.

> THE SHOPKEEPER: *Quelle sorte de biscuits tu veux, gamin?* ('What sort of biscuits do you want, sonny?')
> PHILIP: *Des biscuits* francais. ('*French* biscuits.')

4.5 Code-switching and translation

As we have seen, the bilingual child's development is very similar to that of the monolingual child's, the only difference being that the bilingual has the extra task of distinguishing between the two languages. Directly related to this task are two skills or activities that monolinguals, by definition, can never perform: these are code-switching and translation. For example, Philip (6 yrs) speaking to his father on the phone: '*J'ai été à la piscine aujourd'hui* and I dived for the first time'.

To the outsider, especially to someone who does not speak both the languages in question, code-switching seems confused and confusing and it is very difficult to believe that not only does it follow a set of clear and detailed rules, but that it provides the bilingual with a further communicative means of great expressiveness. Code-switching is a phenomenon that is limited to bilingual situations, where bilinguals talk to other bilinguals and where they can call upon the full communicative resources of both languages. It is always meaningful.

Children soon use it in very subtle ways to express their feelings, emotions or degree of involvement in a conversation, or simply to show that in their family setting they can, if they are tired, use both languages interchangeably and still be understood.

Before we go on to look at different kinds of code-switching, let us just recall two other terms that we have already met and which must not be mistaken for code-switching. The first is *borrowing*, where a word or expression from one language is used in the other but in a 'naturalised' form, that is, it is made to conform with the rules of grammar or pronunciation of the second language. For example:

i) *Je vais faire* checker *ma voiture.* (English 'to check', for *verifier*, is given the French infinitive marker -*er* to convey: 'I'm going to have my car checked'.)
ii) *On est parti en* hovercraft (where the English word for *aéroglisseur* is pronounced *à la française*: 'ovaircraft'). ('We went by hovercraft.')

The second is *language choice*, where the speaker changes from one language to another according to the person she is speaking to. For example:

i) Philip (6 yrs), who is staying in France, wants to phone his English nanny:

> PHILIP: *Maman, quel numéro il faut faire?* ('Mum, what number should I dial?')

> MOTHER: *C'est écrit sur la carte qui est devant toi.* ('It's written on the card in front of you.')
>
> (Philip dials the number)
>
> PHILIP: Hello, Nanny, how are you?

ii) Finn (14 yrs 10 mths) is just off to school:

> MOTHER: *Har du din nyckel?* (Swedish for 'Have you got your key?')
> FINN: *Jo, jag har den – hej, hej.* ('Yes, I've got it, goodbye.')
> MOTHER: *Hej då.* ('Bye, then.')
> FINN (Now addressing his father): Goodbye.
> FATHER: Bye, Finn.

Now let us look at code-switching proper. The most common type of all is probably that which occurs when a speaker cannot find the right word or expression in the language she is speaking, either because she simply can't remember it or because the language in question just doesn't seem to have a satisfactory way of expressing that particular idea, that is, *there isn't a word for it.*

i) Philip (6 yrs 6 mths) is explaining to his mother how to use his newly bought tube of glue: *Tu dévisses le bouchon . . . comme ça . . . et tu* squirt. ('You unscrew the cap . . . like this . . . and you *squirt.*')

ii) Finn: 'We've got a new maths teacher, but he isn't *titulaire . . .* our real maths teacher's on a *stage.*' (Approximate translations: *titulaire* – a teacher who has an established post; *stage* – an in-service training course.)

Another very common type of code-switching is known as *triggering.* A word which is similar in both languages, or the name of a person, place or commercial product, makes the speaker continue in the second language. For example, Philip (4 yrs 1 mth) says to his mother: '*Donne moi encore des* cornflakes, please' ('Give me some more corn-flakes, please') where 'cornflakes', a borrowing, is pronounced *à la française* but nevertheless triggers the switch into English. However, this 'triggered' switching is usually a mechanical accident rather than a deliberate expressive device, little more than a slip, as can be seen by the way speakers return to the right language very rapidly, without even completing the second-language part of the utterance. For example, Emily (14 yrs) said: 'I saw Mme Laurent *qui* was out with Cocky' ('I saw Mme Laurent *who* was out with Cocky' – Cocky is the name of the lady's dog).

When a bilingual quotes in *direct speech*, she can, if she so wishes, attempt to convey not only the person's voice quality and style of speech but also the words the person quoted actually used. For example, Katja (5 yrs 6 mths) is feeling rather pleased with herself, because she has just 'ordered' something in the local shop without asking her mother to buy it for her: 'Dominique said *Madame?* and Mummy said *Une laitue et . . .* and *I* said *et un Malabar!* [a kind of sweet] and they all laughed'.

For quotations in *indirect speech* children usually use the language they habitually use with the person they are speaking to.

Children are also extremely skilful in using switching as a marker of 'solidarity' with the person they are talking to, that is, using the change of language to reinforce the 'closeness' of the relationship. Leopold gives the example of his daughter Hildegard, who at the age of five years and four months considerably intensified the emotional content of what she was saying to coax her father into staying with her when she was in bed with chicken-pox. She said: '*Papa, wenn du das Licht ausmachst*, then I'll be so lonely' ('Daddy, if you put out the light . . .').

Code-switching can also be used to exclude someone from a conversation. However, this is by no means always indicative of a negative attitude towards the people concerned, as these two examples show:

i) Emily (17 yrs 5 mths) is at the table with her German friend Anne, and her parents. The common language is French.

> MOTHER (to Anne): *Tu reprendras un peu de ça?* ('Would you like some more?')
>
> EMILY (to her mother in Swedish): Jag tror inte att hon tycker om det. ('I don't think she likes it.')

Here, Emily was obviously trying to help her friend without embarrassing her.

ii) Philip (7 yrs) to his mother in French (in front of an English guest, urgently): *Maman, j'ai envie de faire pipi.* ('Mummy, I need to have a wee.')

Finally it is also worth noting that code-switching can be used to amplify a point and win an argument. Here is an example. Philip (5 yrs 3 mths) is playing in the garden at home in England.

> MOTHER: *Philip, viens, ton repas est prêt.* ('Philip, come along, your meal is ready.')
>
> PHILIP: . . .
>
> MOTHER: *Phi – lip! Viens ici!* ('Phi – lip! Come here!')
>
> PHILIP: . . .

MOTHER: Philip Harding, come here!
PHILIP: *OK, j'arrive!* ('OK, I'm coming!')

By using the second language, an appeal is made to the outside authority (school, etc.) which it represents to the child. As most parents know, the use of the child's surname has much the same effect. The example illustrates that code-switching is simply an extra resource for communication between parents and children.

Recent research has concentrated on the linguistic constraints that limit code-switching. Researchers have described a number of complex rules which have to be obeyed by bilingual speakers when they switch from one grammatical system to another: interlocking the two systems is not just a matter of stopping speaking in one and starting in another. On the contrary, dovetailing the two systems requires great skill if grammatical 'clashes' are to be avoided and if the overall organisation of the message is to remain clear. There is still much controversy as to how best to describe and account for the details of these operations, but one thing is clear: the more bilingual people are, the better they are at code-switching. At first glance, this may seem very obvious, yet on reflection one sees that it is somewhat surprising that changing from one language to another should be related to one's degree of mastery of *both* languages: 'common sense' would surely have led us to expect switching from a language you do not speak very well to a language in which you are fluent (for example) to be easier than other kinds of switching, but in practice this does not seem to be the case. When people are dominant in one language, they limit their switching to one or two words, for example: '*Leo* un magazine' ('I read a magazine'). On the other hand, people who are highly fluent in both are able to make more complex, in-sentence switches, such as: '*Las palabras* heavy-duty, *bien grandes se me han olvidado*' ('I've forgotten the real big, heavy-duty words'). Both of these examples are taken from an article by Poplack (1980), whose title itself provides a pointed comment on the whole process 'Sometimes I'll start a sentence in English *y termino en Español*' ('. . . and finish it in Spanish').

Parents vary a lot in their attitude to switching, of course. They may themselves try to avoid it, in which case they will tend to prevent their children from doing so, too. On the other hand, they may switch frequently from one language to another, in which case it becomes part of the family's interactive style. As Case Study 4 shows, as long as the parents are consistent, there is no evidence that code-switching has any adverse effects on the bilingual development of children. To the person who sees code-switching as a sign of confusion, this seems surprising, but if it is seen instead as a complex grammatical skill it becomes much more under-standable.

4.6   A 'born translator'?

In this section we will *not* be talking about translating and interpreting as professions. You will find a brief discussion of that topic under *Interpreting and translating* in Part III. Here, we will be discussing 'natural' translation and interpretation in childhood; something bilingual children do from the moment they are able to use both languages independently. Indeed, Harris and Sherwood (1978) go so far as talking of 'translation as an innate skill'. They point out that many children of immigrant parents have to help their parents communicate with speakers of the majority language and that they are not long in realising how much power this gives them. They report the example of the little Italian girl in Canada softening her father's angry outbursts when interpreting for him in his dealings with non-Italians:

> FATHER (to little girl, in Italian): Tell him he's a nitwit.
> LITTLE GIRL (to third party, in English): My father won't accept your offer.
> FATHER (to little girl, in Italian): Why didn't you tell him what I told you?

Similarly, a school teacher from Nanterre told one of the authors that she had eventually been forced to learn some Arabic in order to talk to her pupils' parents, because when she used the children as interpreters to tell the parents they were always late, had disastrous marks or watched too much television, she somehow never got the reactions from the parents that she would have expected!

It must not be thought, however, that translating and interpreting is limited to the children of immigrants. There are also cases like that of the solemn four-year-old American girl, Linda, seen standing on the thresh-old of a flat in Finland, interpreting the conversation between the local postman and her Fullbright Professor father. Children from 'mixed' fami-lies also frequently find themselves in situations where they need to trans-late for monolinguals from different sides of the family or for visitors to their country. (An example is given in Case Study 3.)

Although all bilingual children seem to manage to interpret reasonably well, some are better than others, as is only to be expected. Perhaps it is worth recalling that these tasks do not just require a good control of two languages. They often take place in situations that necessitate specialised knowledge (names of illnesses, food, parts of a car, etc.) and the performance has to be carried out under demanding circumstances, with people looking on, criticising and giving instructions. Apart from linguistic knowledge, then, the quality of the translation will depend on such things as the child's age, previous experience and personality and on the nature of the situation and the relationship between the participants.

Nevertheless, under good conditions, children do seem to enjoy such tasks: any child likes to be needed and approved of socially. Under pressure, the child may resort to something like word-for-word translation (indeed, where the adults can follow some of what the child is saying they may more or less force her to do so) but at other times, the onlooker is struck by the effortless way in which freedom and accuracy are combined:

> FATHER (to an English-speaking French friend): We could take a stroll into Marcillac. It's some kind of special market today (it was 14 July) and we could pick up some fruit and cheese for lunch . . . or we can go by car, as it's so hot.
>
> KATJA (4 yrs 11 mths) (for the benefit of the French friend's daughter): *Et si on allait au village? Il y a un marché parce que nous sommes le quatorze juillet et on pourrait s'acheter des fruits et du fromage pour midi . . . en voiture ou à pied, comme ton père veut parce qu'il fait si chaud.*

('Let's go down to the village. There's a market because it's the 14 July and we could buy some fruit and cheese for midday . . . by car or on foot, as your father likes, because it's so hot.')

The fact that children enjoy translating is confirmed by the way they often do it spontaneously. A favourite trick in which they seem to revel is the word-for-word translation of colloquial expressions, the source of great hilarity:

French expressions:
– *C'est du tout cuit* translates as 'It is all cooked'. The equivalent English expression is 'It's in the bag'.
– *Ça ne casse pas de briques* translates as 'It does not break bricks'. The equivalent English expression is 'Nothing to write home about'.
English expressions:
– 'Pull the other leg.' The equivalent French expression is *Vous me faites marcher* ('You make me walk').
– 'You are driving me up the wall.' The equivalent French expression is *Tu me rends dingue* ('You are driving me mad').

A further example of this is the relish with which film subtitles are criticised (see *Television* in Part III). A favourite game of Edith Harding-Esch's son is to have his mother read aloud to him an English book *in French*, which she finds enormously demanding, while he makes remarks on the bits which have not been translated to his satisfaction. Of course, you can always get your own back: 'Well, *you* try . . .'.

SUCCESSIVE BILINGUALISM

Children can become bilingual or multilingual at any age by adding a language to their first language or languages. Indeed, *successive* bilingualism is one of the most common types among the mobile families who made up such a large proportion of the families we met, as a glance at our case studies will show. The family moves to a new country, usually for reasons connected with the parents' jobs, and the children therefore have to learn a new language. Another major reason for successive bilingualism is that children whose parents speak a non-community language at home will learn their parents' language first, only starting on the community language later as their social contacts widen and in particular when they start going to a playgroup or school (see Case Studies 2 and 10).

It is generally believed that the individual's ability to learn a language gradually diminishes with age. To a very large extent, this belief is based on an uncritical observation of children learning to speak – in fact children put vast amounts of time and effort into mastering a language: where adults do likewise, they seem to learn just as well, pronunciation excepted. In fact, they do *better* in terms of *rate* of acquisition, and not so well in terms of eventual outcome.

But the belief is also based on the undeniable fact that younger people do seem to acquire native-like accents, whereas older people seldom lose their foreign accents. Such observations have been used in support of the 'critical period hypothesis'. According to this hypothesis, human beings are programmed for the acquisition of language between birth and puberty. After that time, the brain begins to lose its plasticity and our ability to learn a language 'naturally' diminishes correspondingly.

This hypothesis has been seriously undermined since it was first formulated. It has been shown, for example, that lateralisation of the brain, (which was supposed to be concomitant with the end of the period) in fact occurs much earlier. It has also been demonstrated that adults can in fact learn to discriminate between slightly different sounds faster and better than children, as well as reproducing them more accurately. If it is a fact that adolescent and adult bilinguals do usually retain a foreign accent, it looks very much as if the reasons have nothing to do with the neurological development and organisation of the brain, but rather that it results from their need (conscious or unconscious) to show that they are 'different', to proclaim and protect their individual and social identity. (Those monolinguals who hang on to traces of their original accent years after they have moved away from the town or district in question are doing exactly the same thing.) This may seem nonsense to parents who have seen their children learn a second language in a matter of months while they still struggle along after a number of years. But if we actually compare the learning opportunities available to children and adults both quantitatively and qualitatively, we will see that children usually have enormous advantages: if young children learn languages it is because the whole of society is organised in such a way as to teach children languages while they are young and because children have little else to do to distract them from the task. A survey of all the research and evidence (Singleton, 1989) shows clearly that age, in itself, is not particularly relevant to success in language learning, whereas motivation and opportunity are. But researchers such as Scovel (1988) maintain that adults' inability to self-monitor their accents when they have acquired their second language after about age ten argues for the strong version of the critical period hypothesis.

The importance of a learner's *attitude* towards a new linguistic community is central. A child who has a positive attitude towards the new community is obviously going to try to make friends: this in turn is going to make demands on his learning abilities and will also increase his motivation to learn. If the child feels rejected or ignored, on the other hand, he will not attempt to forge links with the new community and will consequently have a very low motivation. He himself will then reduce the number of occasions that would require him to communicate in the new language. These factors have been shown to be far more important than intellectual capacity or language aptitude in predicting whether a particular individual will become a successful bilingual or not.

4.7   Is a second language learnt in the same way as the first?

There is a sense in which this question seems trivial. Of course *not* seems the obvious answer. When we learn a first language we use it to acquire the notions, ideas and concepts that help us think. When we learn a second language, those notions and thoughts are already there and, for better or worse, are going to come between the learner and the new language. You cannot learn a first language twice.

Nowadays, nobody denies this (with the exception of a few commercial language schools). However, opinions are divided as to just how important this point is. Some linguists and psychologists think that it is crucial, since in order to learn anything we make use of what we already know. Thus, they argue, the knowledge of our first language influences strongly and at all levels what we learn of the second language, that is, there is strong interference to start with which gradually diminishes, all the elements which we had transferred from our first language being gradually replaced by elements of the second. This is the 'transfer' position.

More recently, it has been maintained that 'there is a unity of process that characterises all language acquisition and . . . this unity of process reflects similar strategies of language acquisition' (McLaughlin, 1978). In other words, despite interference from the first language, the learning techniques we adopt and the stages we pass through are similar in both cases.

Evidence for both the 'transfer' and the 'developmental' positions is based essentially on the analysis of errors made by second language learners. Earlier studies stressed the importance of errors due to interference from the first language, but a number of later studies showed that not only could errors not be predicted from one's knowledge of the first language but, more important, that learners who have completely different mother tongues produce the same sorts of errors, and that these were on the whole very similar to the errors made by children acquiring that language as a first language.

More recently, researchers have taken a much more balanced position and shown that both factors ('transfers' and 'strategies') interact in extremely complex ways in the course of language acquisition. Indeed, while theoretical issues keep being debated (Paradis and Genesee, 1996) leading researchers like Fillmore and Keller-Cohen have abandoned an entirely linguistic approach, focusing instead on the child's learning *behaviour*, that is, how the child learns the social, cognitive and linguistic strategies used in acquiring a language in a natural environment. They have shown that in the first 'interactional' stage, the child establishes *social* relationships with the speakers of the second language: during this stage, heavy reliance on fixed formulas and non-verbal communication is to be expected. In the second stage, the child concentrates on communicating and starts analysing the formulas which have up till then been learnt as wholes in order to build up new sentences with the elements. The third stage is when the child checks systematically that the forms she uses are correct.

Some of the *cognitive strategies* described by Fillmore will sound all too familiar to readers who have ever had to 'manage' abroad in a foreign language:

– Assume that what people are saying is directly relevant to the situation at hand or to what they or you are experiencing.
– Get some expressions you understand and start talking.
– Look for recurring parts in the formulas you know.
– Make the most of what you've got.
– Work on big things: save the details for later.

Three *social strategies* will sound no less familiar:

– Join a group and act as if you understand what is going on, even if you don't.
– Give the impression, with a few well-chosen words, that you can speak the language.
– Count on your friends for help.

Keller-Cohen (1979) insists on the fact that:

> Prior experience with language contributes to a child's second language learning by providing [him or her] with heuristics for *searching and organising* linguistic data and with knowledge about that language.

These would include such techniques as:

– Pay attention to the order of linguistic elements.
– Look for sequences.
– Don't interrupt or rearrange sequences.
– Represent information simply.

If such 'strategies' do not explain at all what the language acquisition process is, they are none the less likely to make very good sense to parents and to be helpful to them, because they stress the importance of providing the child with friends with whom to build up social relations and to play. Such strategies also help us understand why it is difficult for the parents to learn the new language as quickly and as well as their children: there are lots of situations where it is simply impossible for adults to 'pretend you understand' or to 'save the details for later'. If learning is sometimes hard on the children, it is likely to be absolute hell for their parents!

BILINGUALISM AND INTELLIGENCE

> Almost no general statements are warranted by research on the effects of bilingualism. It has not been demonstrated that bilingualism has positive or negative consequences for intelligence, linguistic skills, educational attainment, emotional adjustment or cognitive functioning. In almost every case, the findings of research are either contradicted by other research or can be questioned on methodological grounds. The one statement that is supported by research findings is that command of a second language makes a difference if a child is tested in that language – a not very surprising finding.
>
> (McLaughlin, 1978)

We have two reasons for quoting the above passage. The first is to show that attempts to relate bilingualism scientifically to other intellectual skills have regularly foundered because we cannot satisfactorily define those skills, let alone measure them and compare them to other skills. In particular, the study of bilingualism has trailed in the wake of the study of 'intelligence', following every twist and turn in its course, so that bilingualism has been judged 'good' or 'bad' according to the nature of the tests in question, which were almost never specifically developed for the study of bilingualism as such.

The second is that the judgement on bilingualism summarised in this quotation leaves parents free, if they so wish, to help their children benefit from the potentially enormous *social* benefits of bilingualism. For if it has never been proved one way or another that the effects of bilingualism are positive or negative from the intellectual point of view, it is a matter of daily experience that knowing two or more languages is of immediate practical, and social, value.

In this section, we will be discussing briefly some of the major research studies on bilingualism in relation to intelligence or intellectual development. What is the influence of bilingualism on intelligence? Does a child risk becoming less intelligent if we bring her up with two languages rather than one? Psychologists have tried to answer these questions for over half a century, yet even the subject shows that they have been far more concerned with the nature of intelligence than with the nature of bilingualism. This is a main reason why research in this area yields contradictory results depending on the type of tests used.

Earlier studies indicated that bilingual children had lower IQs than monolingual children. For instance Saer (1923) tested Welsh / English children and found that not only were the bilinguals' IQs lower in rural areas, but that the difference between monolinguals and bilinguals increased with each year between the ages of seven and eleven. A number of other studies confirmed these findings. The result of these studies was a widespread belief that 'bilingualism is bad for you', which just happens to confirm the assumptions of the monolingual majorities in Europe, and the USA (where it also gave 'scientific' support to the social concept of the 'melting pot' in which ethnic differences were to disappear).

However, a number of methodological weaknesses in intelligence tests slowly became apparent. In particular, it became clear that the socio-economic background of monolingual children had to be taken into account. When this was done, it was observed that the discrepancies between monolingual children and bilingual children had also narrowed or even disappeared. Other flaws that slowly came to light were a failure to take *degree* of bilingualism into account and the fact that the tests themselves were very 'verbal' in nature – the language in question being that of the monolingual majority, of course. It cannot be repeated often enough that to compare a bilingual's results with a monolingual's in this kind of test does not make much sense: if the bilingual is to be penalised a certain number of points for weaknesses in that language, why should the monolingual not be penalised equally heavily for her 'weaknesses' in the second language?

Even these earlier tests showed that if *non-verbal* measures were used (that is, questions and exercises that could be set and accomplished without recourse to language as such – shapes, numbers and so on) bilinguals' scores were as good as monolinguals'. For example, Arsenian (1937) studied 2,000 students in New York City using two tests that required mimed instructions (the mind boggles!) and could detect no significant cause-effect relationship between bilingualism and IQ. It became clearer than ever that linguistic fluency and class background influenced results in IQ testing in general and by the 1950s, the use of the Stanford-Binet Test and Stanford Achievement Tests on bilinguals was discontinued.

In 1953, Darcy undertook a major review of bilingual studies. Of the 40 investigations he catalogued and analysed, he found only two that showed any kind of direct relationship between fluency in two languages and intelligence (and those turned out to suffer from the methodological flaws mentioned earlier).

The swing of the pendulum continued and in 1962 Peal and Lambert published the first major study to show that bilinguals as a group performed *better* than monolinguals on both verbal and non-verbal intelligence tests. Their subjects were ten year olds from six different schools in

Montreal and the comparison was between French / English bilinguals and French monolinguals. Apart from the results in IQ tests, the bilingual children were also better academically at school and they were more favourably inclined to English Canadians than their French monolingual peers. Peal and Lambert concluded that the key factor in the bilinguals' success may have been the cognitive skills which are commonly associated with bilingualism, in particular mental flexibility and concept formation.

However, the authors were very cautious about the cause–effect relationship between intelligence and bilingualism. As argued by Ellen Bialystock, the difficulty resides in defining the constructs 'intelligence' and 'bilingualism' in a satisfactory way. To ask 'What is the influence of bilingualism on intelligence?' or 'What is the influence of intelligence on bilingualism?' may be the wrong questions. Obviously, there must be dull bilinguals and clever bilinguals, and the clever bilingual's intelligence will show up in her bilingual ability, but the cause–effect relationship between the two was not demonstrated by Peal and Lambert and has not been since.

Most studies reporting that bilingualism had 'negative effects' were carried out on children from minority language groups who have to learn the majority language whether they like it or not and who, very often, have not reached a very high degree of proficiency in their mother tongue when they start the second language in school. In contrast, most of the studies reporting 'positive effects' were made in societies where bilingualism is encouraged, where the languages concerned are both high-status languages and where the parents of the children tested have relatively high socio-economic class.

As a consequence of their own research results, Lambert and Peal pleaded for a shift of emphasis 'from looking for favourable or unfavourable effects of bilingualism on intelligence to an inquiry into the basic nature of these effects'. Since the 1960s that plea has been heeded by more and more linguists and psychologists. Rather than asking whether the bilingual's intelligence is better or worse than the monolingual's, researchers have tried to discover and describe its specific characteristics: in what ways is it different?

The current answer to this question, according to Bialystock (2001), is that the most consistent empirical finding about the cognition of bilingual children is their ability to focus their attention on what is essential in a task or problem, and not to be distracted by misleading information. There is no evidence that bilinguals excel in either conceptual analysis or in attentional control, but their advantage is in the interaction between the demands of these processes. This result is exciting for neuropsychologists because the development of inhibition of attention attributed to the pre-frontal lobe in the brain seems to play a central role in cognitive function-ing, and its decline, associated with a decrease in ability to achieve intentional thought, is symptomatic of ageing. For the parents of bilingual children, it will not come as a surprise to hear that childhood bilingualism seems to have a deep influence on intellectual development and it will be reassuring to know that any difference identified so far, however small, appears to be cognitively advantageous.

If you are considering the possibilities of becoming a bilingual family, you should, by now, have a better idea of what to expect. In the following chapter, you will find a list of the questions you should ask yourselves before making your decision.

CHAPTER FIVE

What will influence your decision whether to bring up your children as bilinguals?

QUESTIONS YOU SHOULD ASK YOURSELF

In Chapter 2, we saw that bilingualism exhibits extremely varied patterns throughout the world and that bilingual individuals live in a variety of linguistic situations. This is why the decision to bring children up as bilinguals from birth, or to switch to or add another language later on (during an extended stay abroad, for example) is rarely a clear-cut problem with only a single possible solution. Here are some of the most important factors involved in determining whether or not to go bilingual.

5.1 What is your own language background and history?

If they are bilingual themselves, parents are likely to have very strong views on the matter. In our experience, most of them will opt for bilingualism as the only 'natural' or 'sensible' thing to do. However, it can work both ways: parents whose language recalls a country or a period they wish to reject or forget may decide that they will drop it. This is understandable enough, though it may be a decision that will be greatly regretted by their children and even their grandchildren. Andrea's grandfather escaped from northern Italy early last century to avoid conscription into the Austrian army. In London, he became a leader of the Italian *Fascisti*. His large and socially mobile family did not bring up a single one of his grandchildren speaking any Italian, one of the reasons being their clear wish to break with such an embarrassing past. (The grandfather was interned, although that was the cause of more anger than shame.) Andrea was brought up in the States but later returned to Europe and spent a year in Italy studying the dialect spoken by her grandparents.

5.2 What language(s) do you speak to one another?

This question will very often determine whether it will be *easy* to bring up the children bilingually or not. If the parents were previously in the habit of talking to each other in the language of the outside community, then the parent who wishes to pass on his or her other language to the child will clearly have to put a lot of time and effort into the child's language education. If, on the other hand, the parents use a language between themselves at home which is not that of the outside community, they have to be ready to accept the consequences of running a 'foreign home'. For the parents themselves this will probably not have any major consequences on their social lives: English people are not going to be surprised that someone they know is German (and who speaks good English anyway) should speak German at home with his children in, say, Birmingham. It is only when the children start going to the local playgroup or bring their friends home that 'social' obstacles begin to crop up. (Though, with a little tact, these can be overcome.)

A third and increasingly common case is that of parents who use a language together which is not the native tongue of either of them. Kurt and Soraja, a German scientist and his Pakistani wife, have settled for English as their common language, as have Egon (a Dane) and Annja (a Finn). Yet neither couple lives in an English-speaking country (they live in Germany and Denmark respectively). So whatever decision these couples make, the language pattern of the family is going to be complicated: if each of them decides to speak their own language to the children, they will end up in a tri-lingual situation (and the children might be forgiven for thinking that every pair of human beings speaks a different language from any other pair!).

A variation on this situation is the language pattern established in Philip and Marianne Riley's home: both parents speak their mother tongue (English and Swedish) to their three children, but communication between the parents is uniquely in English. The community language, French, is never used between members of the family at home, except occasionally in the presence of visitors. The children speak English or Swedish to one another.

5.3 How do you use your respective languages?

In the examples we have mentioned so far, the parents stuck to a single language when speaking to one another. But at least two other arrangements can and do occur. The first is where each of the parents continues speaking their mother tongue. For example, the father says something in German, the mother replies in French, the father comes back in German, the mother continues in French, and so on. (An example of this arrangement will be found in Case Study 4.)

The other possibility, and quite a common solution in practice it would seem, is for the person who speaks first to determine the choice of language. For example, if it is the German father who initiates an exchange, the whole exchange is held in German; if the mother, the conversation takes place in French. However, it is also very frequent for parents who do not have the same mother tongue, but who are highly proficient in both, to switch quite happily from one to the other when in conversation with one another. There is nothing wrong with this, but parents who do so must realise that it is going to have an influence on the way the children will learn to exchange with other members of the family (see Case Study 4).

5.4 Who is going to look after your child?

In very general terms, the common-sense idea that the more you use a language, the better you get at it, holds true. This precept also seems to apply to two languages, with the logical corollary that our mastery of each of the two will be in direct proportion to the time we are exposed to them. In other words, if a child speaks English for seven hours a day and French for one, there is a strong possibility that his English will be, let us say, several times better than his French, since these things cannot be measured exactly.

Several years ago one of the writers of this book was approached by an Englishman in his late twenties who had the following complaint: he had agreed with his French wife that they should bring up their child bilingually in English and French. However, 'it hadn't worked'. The child now spoke French as his mother tongue in the literal sense, but his English was so poor that the father found himself obliged to talk to his own son in French. Since he had first been persuaded to try bilingualism by a radio broadcast given by us, he phoned to lay the blame squarely at our door.

A subsequent interview revealed that the boy's upbringing was left almost entirely to his mother and grandmother, partly because of the distribution of roles and tasks in that family, partly because the father worked extremely long hours (he was regularly out of the house twelve hours every working day) when, indeed, he was not actually away on business trips. Expressed in these bald terms the father's disappointment seems naive. Yet he was an intelligent man and a doting father: he simply had not appreciated the extent to which a commitment to bilingualism would call into question his roles as husband and father. It is not just chance that the best published case studies of bilingualism – as compared with studies of first language acquisition – have been written by linguist fathers who, apart from their professional interest and natural curiosity as regards what was happening, also spent an enormous amount of time interacting and talking with their children. The technical literature on bilingual children constitutes a reappraisal of the father's role in the family. Establishing a bilingual home is very much about sharing the children's education fully between both parents, and we are talking as much about walks, baths and bedtime stories as about decisions concerning what school the child will attend.

Many parents find it quite impossible to use anything other than their mother tongue with their babies, even when they had firmly made up their minds to do quite the opposite before the child arrived. In particular, we know of a number of mothers who had agreed 'rationally' to drop their native language but who, when it came to the first lullaby, knew they could never do any such thing.

Another reaction is reported in Case Study 5, which is about an Austrian / French couple living in Brazil. The German-speaking mother reported that she went through a period when she found it difficult to speak at all to her new-born son because 'it just seemed ridiculous to be speaking German in Brazil to someone who could not understand a word of what [she] was saying'. Such unpredictable reactions cannot easily be explained and may force the parents to revise their plans.

If both parents work, the person(s) looking after the child is / are obviously going to play a very important role in the child's language development. Where this person speaks the language of the community, and receives the child into her own home or playgroup, this may well tip the balance in favour of the establishment of a 'foreign home', so that the child gets used to the pattern of one language at home, another language outside. On the other hand, if the parents call on the help of an au pair, or some similar person who comes to the child's home, it may well be easier to establish a pattern of one person / one language. This pattern has been shown to be generally favourable to the separation of languages by children. However, it is still not as simple as it seems, since, to continue with our example, an au pair comes to a country to learn that country's language. A French au pair, given the choice of speaking French or English with a child in England, will feel very tempted to choose English. Even where this is not the case, there will be many occasions where one of the languages will be used as a second language. Generally, as both Döpke (1992) and Tokuhama-Espinosa (2001) emphasize, parents need to know that raising children bilingually requires a lot of thought and effort.

5.5 What are your attitudes towards your own language?

Parents vary greatly in their attitude towards their own language and it is this which usually determines how committed they are to the idea of a bilingual home. Earlier, we mentioned the cases of parents who felt they just *had* to speak to their children in their mother tongue. In fact, they may feel this way with all members of their family, not just babies. Even people who have settled abroad, who are living there happily and speak the foreign language fluently, can miss their own language badly. To speak to people who are close to them in a second language is something they find unbearable; they feel that they are not themselves, that their identity is threatened. (Much is made of the 'identity problems' of bilinguals, but in our view the person who has to give up their mother tongue is in a far worse position.) Other people really do not seem to mind leaving their first language behind, and sometimes even enjoy having it as a sort of 'secret garden' for themselves, in which case their commitment to bilingualism in their family will be much weaker. Obviously, the only people who can decide on this matter are the individuals concerned, and provided they are happy with the outcome, no harm is done whichever way they decide. It is worth remembering, though, especially if you are young and perhaps just married, that the decision is an important one, since, once taken, it is difficult to reverse. It will probably be with you, quite literally, for the rest of your lives.

The parents' attitude towards their own language is perhaps more important than the objective situation of that language in the foreign society. This is especially true of women isolated in some way, either because they live in rural communities or in high-rise flats. If you live in an out-of-the-way village, it really doesn't matter very much whether, objectively, the language you speak has 'high status' or not. The signs that yours is a high-status language, for example, that it is a subject offered in secondary schools, that heads of state speak it, that there is a television course for adult beginners and so on, can all seem pretty remote to a mother whose main company is one or more under-fives: and it is precisely in this period that the children are learning to talk. During these years, it is the parents' views as to what is important and valuable that count, not those of the outside society. This can mean that parents drop a language that is valued by their own society, but it can also mean deliberately introducing a second language into the home, simply because the parents have such high regard for it. An example of this situation is reported in Saunders' (1982) book, *Bilingual Children*, where he describes the successful bilingual acquisition of German by his sons in Australia. The decision to establish a bilingual home was taken largely because the parents loved German, which was a second language for both of them, and where there was no external pressure to introduce and maintain it.

5.6   What contacts do you have with the rest of the family?

One of the most common and understandable reasons why parents wish their children to become bilingual is that they want them to be able to talk to their grandparents and to their aunts, uncles and cousins. Family visits and holidays can be awkward occasions if some relatives simply cannot communicate with others. In our experience, it can be particularly hard on grandparents to have grandchildren with whom they cannot communicate in their own language. Big hugs and boxes of chocolates simply do not go very far. This is why parents who decide against bilingualism, because they 'want to keep the family united' or 'to preserve the fabric of the family' can find that the result of their decision is counter-productive. The same can even apply to cases where the parents decide to introduce the second language only after one has already been well established, in order to avoid the presumed dangers of the simultaneous acquisition of two languages. In a case reported by Saunders, the parents had required the grandmother not to address the child in question until he was almost two years old. Even if there were some linguistic justification for such a measure (and we do not believe this to be the case) the strain placed on family relationships is the opposite of the result that this strategy aimed to achieve in the first place.

Close contacts with grandparents and cousins 'back home' are very important. In many cases they are the first time the child fully realises that people other than his mother and father speak the language in question.

Can you picture the mixture of delight and amazement on a four-year-old boy's face, telling his parents struggling with their luggage in Victoria Station on Christmas Eve: 'Dad, Mum! That policeman, he spoke to me *in English*!' Such experiences allow the children themselves to become aware of just what being bicultural means and to do so in a progressive manner and in the context of rich and loving relationships. For example, it may all start with the horrified realisation that your French grandad not only doesn't know what tomato ketchup is, but he doesn't even *care*!

From the purely linguistic point of view, cousins are often the main source of contact with the mother's or father's language as spoken by members of the child's own generation: what a delight to come back with a set of expressions that not even your parents understand, such as *Maintenant, on plouffe* ('Now, let's count out'), *Je vais me faire tricard!* ('He / she is going to give me hell!'), 'He / she is fit' (i.e. 'sexually attractive'), 'He / she is a minger' (i.e. 'ugly'), or 'Look at her bling bling' (extravagant jewellery in Afro-American media culture).

Family relationships vary enormously, obviously, and many of the affective and psychological factors involved go well beyond the competence of the present writers, even though such factors may play a direct and important role in decisions concerning bilingualism. A none too rare situation is that of the parent who has left his own country precisely because he did not get on well with his own family and wanted to break away from it. One does not need to be a psychoanalyst to see that in such circumstances the decision to establish a bilingual home will often go along with a desire to resolve personal problems.

It is important to remember that whatever the decisions they may come to about bilingualism, parents cannot hope to educate their children without revealing to them their attitudes towards their own families and parents, and their country and community of origin. And in those cases where the parent wants to forget about such things, the child is almost certain, sooner or later, to want to know why.

5.7   What are the languages concerned?

Although most studies of the simultaneous acquisition of two languages deal with pairs of languages that are related, there are a certain number of studies that deal with unrelated languages. By and large, these studies show that from the point of view of their *structure*, the particular pair of languages concerned does not make much difference to the eventual outcome. This is the conclusion indicated by studies of Swedish / Finnish bilinguals (Swedish is an Indo-European language, Finnish is not). The conclusion is supported by Burling (an English-speaking anthropologist whose son became a 'native speaker' of Garo, a Tibeto-Burman language spoken in Assam) as well as by Smith's studies involving Chinese and English (Chinese is a tone language, English is not). Structural differences do have an influence on the actual mechanics of the acquisition process, but they do not determine whether or to what extent bilingualism will be achieved.

What *does* make a considerable difference, however, is the *relative status* of the pair of languages in question, both within the family and within society at large. This is where the 'official' patterns of bilingualism mentioned in Chapter 2 can have a direct influence on the decision taken by the parents. The question often boils down to, 'Is it worth it?' That is, is the language in question sufficiently widespread, useful, respected and so on, to justify the effort involved in its maintenance (see Case Study 6).

It would be unrealistic of us to pretend that, in terms of public attitudes, all languages are equal. The fact is that some of them are very much more equal than others. This inequality is due to public perceptions of their usefulness and prestige but also to differing attitudes to the speakers of a particular language, which may vary from admiration to contempt.

It is not easy for parents to dissociate themselves from value judgements of this kind. Dropping a 'small' language in favour of a 'big' one can be made to seem a matter of common sense or of some inevitable historical development, particularly if the 'big' language is the father's and the 'little' one the mother's. However, parents should keep in mind the fact that the social benefits of bilingualism (such as being able to talk to Grandad or to share a cultural in-joke with Mum) have little or nothing to do with the world-wide utility or otherwise of the language in question.

Parents who do decide to keep up a language whose value and use is not generally recognised must be prepared, though, to meet a certain amount of incomprehension or prejudice which, over the years, may be very discouraging and demand an extra amount of effort and will-power.

In general terms, then, this will not be the case for languages that are perceived as having *high prestige* by native speakers and / or others. High prestige languages are those that are regarded as world languages, or that have some special economic, religious or cultural value: English, French and Spanish are the most obvious examples, but languages such as Arabic, Chinese and Hebrew should also be included in this category.

Middle prestige languages are seen as having less significance, but are usually still prestigious or personally important enough to merit the effort of maintenance, thus allowing for a good self-image in the family. Finnish in certain areas of North America is one example of this.

Low prestige languages, however enthusiastically they may be promoted by various agencies, tend to be seen as old-fashioned, dying out, the languages of the uneducated, irrelevant to the modern world. Many so-called 'regional' languages fall into this category: examples which come to mind are Gaelic in Scotland, Andaluz in Spain and Occitan in France.

Parents should be aware that their attempts to bring up their children bilingually will often be evaluated by outsiders according to the relative positions of their languages on this scale of prestige. Few people will criticise the value (as against the practicability) of bringing up children as French / English or German / Spanish bilinguals. But as soon as we begin to move down the scale to, for example, English / Gaelic, German / Finnish or French / Occitan, there will be a reaction of the 'Is it worth it?' type. The answer is, yes, it may well be: not in terms of world statistics (and the various prejudices and tensions for which these are often used to camouflage or rationalise) but in terms of the individual family's social life and of the bilingual child's cultural inheritance (see Case Study 6).

Differences in status between languages clearly influence the parents' decision as to whether or not to establish a bilingual home, but they also act directly on the *climate* in which the children will become bilingual and the *variety of means* available to help the parents in their task. Although the English / French bilingual child living in England may find himself regarded as something of a pedagogical problem both by parents and school, the simple fact that all the other children have to learn French will be enough to make belonging to the French community and speaking French a source of pride. But when the child's home language is simply unknown at school, or is mistaken for another language, the child may well be discouraged even in cases of elective bilingualism. The child from Pakistan who discovers that people are not sure about the difference between Pakistan and India, and whose schoolmates, and even teachers, tell him in good faith that he 'speaks Indian', will find his self-confidence eroded and will begin to question his parents' values and language. This tendency grows as the child's peer group increases in importance in his life.

Children often hate to 'be different' and have been known to request their parents not to speak the home language to them in front of their friends. These are times when only parental support and affection can help the child overcome what are usually temporary difficulties (see *Refusing to speak the language* in Part III).

5.8   What means of support are available for maintaining the language?

It is far easier to obtain children's books and cassettes in some languages than in others. For example, materials suitable for children are available in all the main European languages and often it is not even necessary to go back to or order them from the 'home' country. On the other hand, if the language is 'rare', acquiring even the simplest of materials can be difficult and the same is true as regards sharing facilities with other parents, or organising a little library or playgroup. This can also apply when the language is by no means a rare one but the parents are isolated from contacts with the home country or members of the home community.

From these two points of view at least (that is, the general climate and the availability of materials) there *are* languages that are more difficult than others to maintain in the home. These difficulties can and have been overcome, of course, but there is no miracle cure: in the main it depends entirely on how much time parents can or will spend with their children.

5.9   Would you have to change the way you communicate with one another?

As many readers will no doubt know from their own experience, it is extremely difficult to change the language (or languages) in which you communicate with someone once a habit has been established. The language used becomes, as it were, a definition of the relationship and the receptacle of all the common knowledge and shared experience. Changing the language feels like a denial of the past, like starting again from scratch with a stranger. The deeper and more firmly established the relationship and the habits, the more difficult it is to change and many couples have found it quite impossible. 'It just doesn't feel right' is the sort of thing they say: a vague enough expression, but one that seems to touch on fundamental issues of relationships, role and personality. In theory, there is nothing to stop such a change taking place: in practice, though, it just does not seem to happen.

For this reason, any attempt to establish bilingualism that involves a change in the language or languages in which the parents address one another is, in our experience, most unlikely to succeed. (In fact, we know of no successful example.) For example, if a German / English couple living in England habitually communicate with one another in English, they are unlikely to be able to change to using German on the arrival of a baby. This certainly does not mean that they cannot establish a bilingual home. It means that the particular pattern (all members of the family speaking German all the time at home) would seem to be the most difficult one to establish. But obviously other patterns are available to them, for example, the German-speaking parent communicating with the children in German, the English-speaking parent talking to them in English, and the parents continuing to speak English to one another.

We believe this to be an important point, because failure to adapt the pattern of bilingualism to the already-existing language pattern seems to be a regular cause of cases where 'We tried bilingualism but it didn't work'.

REACHING A DECISION

5.10   Some 'golden rules'

When all is said and done, the decision is yours. Or at least, it should be; don't let outsiders, whether family or 'authorities', push you around. Remember, you know best. Remember, too, that there is no evidence that bilingualism does any intellectual harm (if anything, the reverse is true) and that bilingualism can be of great social benefit. This brings us back to your situation, which will obviously determine whether or not there are short- and long-term social benefits to be gained by your child's being bilingual. Will he be able to communicate with grandparents, cousins, friends and visitors? Will you be going 'home' either for holidays or at the end of a contract? What are your plans for his education? Only you can know and decide on these matters: we have tried to indicate factors that you would do well to take into account but, ultimately, the effort and (in many cases) the rewards, are up to you.

For the moment, then, we will limit ourselves to a few general pieces of advice – most of it obvious, but still important and so worth making explicit – in the hope that you will find in the various other sections of this book (particularly the last two) the more detailed recommendations that you might be looking for.

First, and most obviously: *the child's happiness comes first.* If ever you should really come to the decision that trying to 'be bilingual' is in some sense a source of misery, you should seriously reconsider your position. However, we have not so far in our investigations found any such example (see *Refusing to speak the language* in Part III). On the other hand, there are very many cases indeed where putting the child's happiness first means that you should make every effort to encourage and maintain bilingualism, since he will *need* (in the widest sense) his second language in order to live a full and satisfying childhood. Nothing might be sadder than, for example, 'losing' half your family.

A corollary to this is that the child should never be teased or embarrassed in any way about his linguistic performance, particularly in his weaker language (yes, there will almost certainly be a relatively weaker language). This includes protecting the child when he is asked to 'perform' by adults and by avoiding comparisons between his performance (especially in his weaker language) and that of monolingual children. Of course, a child should never be punished for making mistakes; as far as possible you should avoid correcting your child overtly too (see *Correcting* in Part III) especially if this means constantly interrupting him.

Above all *talk* to your child, and this applies to both father and mother. Provide him with the richest linguistic environment possible (songs, playgroup, books, television, holidays, visitors, games) in *both* languages.

Be consistent in your linguistic behaviour with your child, but remember that there are many different ways of being consistent: one parent, one language; a holiday language and a round-the-year language; a weekday language and a Sunday language; the first one to speak chooses the language; everyone speaking their preferred language. You will find examples of all these arrangements in the case studies. Remember, too, that to be consistent often requires considerable effort and patience on your part.

Finally, *play it down*. For most bilingual children and their parents, as we have seen, their linguistic situation is just part of their life. It is a part that can be useful, fun and interesting, but it is still something that they share with the majority of the world's population (see section 2.4) and therefore neither a cause for concern nor anything to shout about.

5.11   Assess your own situation

Below you will find a questionnaire to help you assess the situation of your own family. When you have read it, you may find it useful to look back over this chapter. *What will influence your decision whether to bring up your children as bilinguals?* Our aim is to help you make that decision a conscious and realistic one that takes into account the specific characteristics of your own situation.

Questionnaire

The aim of this questionnaire is to help you think about your situation in the light of the issues discussed in the preceding chapters. Not all the questions will apply to all readers, and, of course, there are no *right* answers. If you make a couple of photocopies of the questionnaire, you and your partner could fill them in separately and then discuss your answers.

1 What languages do you speak?

	Language	Skills	How did you learn it?
You	1.............................	SURW	1..............................
	2.............................	SURW	2..............................
	3.............................	SURW	3..............................
	4.............................	SURW	4..............................
Your partner	1.............................	SURW	1..............................
	2.............................	SURW	2..............................
	3.............................	SURW	3..............................
	4.............................	SURW	4..............................

(S = Speak, U = Understand, R = Read, W = Write)

2 What language(s) do you speak to one another? If more than one, what is it that determines your choice at any given time or makes you change from one to the other? Has this always been the case? If not, what brought about the change?

....

....

....

3 Were you yourselves brought up as bilinguals? If so, in what languages?

You	Your partner
....	....
....	....
....	....
....	....

4 Will you have any choice as to whether to bring your children up bilingually or not? Why not?

....

....

....

5 In general terms, do you think bilingualism is:
good/bad/neither
natural/unnatural/neither
easy/difficult/neither
useful/a hindrance/neither
pleasant/unpleasant/neither

6 Have you already made any plans about whether or not to bring your children up bilingually? What are those plans? What are their main advantages? What might upset them? Or will you just play it by ear?

....

....

....

7 Have you already taken advice (from books, people, etc.) about bilingualism? If so, what was it?

....

....

....

Do you agree with it? Do you intend to follow it? If not, why not?

....

....

....

8 Are the languages in question equally useful:

  – in your family?   ....

  – in the world?   ....

  Do you have any strong likes or dislikes as regards those languages?

  ....

  ....

  ....

9 If you decide to bring up your children bilingually will you have to
  – change the language(s) you speak to one another?

  ....

  ....

  ....

  – learn to speak and/or understand a new language?

  ....

  ....

  ....

10 Do you know any other bilingual families? Are they in your situation?
   Are you in contact?

  ....

  ....

  ....

11 How do you envisage keeping up your children's non-community
   language(s), that is, the language(s) *not* spoken by most of the people
   around them? (Visits to and from relatives, visits home, books and
   cassettes, special schools, television, etc.)

  ....

  ....

  ....

12 Do you think you would like having bilingual children or would it be something of a nuisance or a mixed blessing?

....

....

....

13 Do you speak as a first language the language of the community in which you will be bringing up your children?

....

....

....

14 Try to diagram the family situation you envisage. If there is more than one possible arrangement, what do the differences between them depend on?

II

Case studies: a number of bilingual families, and how they did it

In this section, you will find eighteen case studies in which we have tried to paint the 'linguistic family portraits' of a variety of bilingual families. These studies are based on observation and extensive interviewing. In the preparation of the second edition, we have been able to contact some of the children whose parents had been interviewed nearly twenty years ago and we asked them for their thoughts about their bilingual experience. Quotes from them have been added at the end of the relevant case studies. We wish to express here our gratitude for their kind cooperation.

What we hope to do is to describe to present or future parents of bilingual children a representative selection of the arrangements that the families in question have found to be feasible and practical in their particular situations. By comparing the descriptions given here with your own circumstances, you will be able to take advantage of the accumulated experience which these studies contain and to make more informed decisions.

Do not be surprised, though, if you do not find a case study that corresponds exactly to your own situation. As we have tried to show, bilingualism is a complex phenomenon and the changes that can be rung on it seem infinite. None the less, we do believe that these cases do cover, at least in outline, the most common and successful forms of family bilingualism. Above all, remember – you are not alone!

To help clarify the established pattern of language choice in a number of the families described in the case studies, we have drawn diagrams. These show:

- On the left, the language(s) used by the parents together.
- Horizontally, the language(s) used by the father and mother when addressing the children.
- On the right, the language(s) used between the children.

Note that these do not necessarily show the pattern that occurs when both parents are talking to the children at the same time.

Case Study 1: English as a 'father tongue'

Peter and Anne Marie are an English / French couple living in Eastern France. Peter, who originally qualified as an industrial chemist in his native Britain, came to France in 1969. He now works as a teacher of scientific English to French engineering and mathematics students. Anne Marie was a teacher of German, but has not worked for the last few years, in order to look after their two young children, Carine (aged 8) and Lydia (aged 3).

Both parents are extremely positive in their attitude towards bilingualism, although they never took a conscious decision to bring up the children bilingually. The mother had had first-hand experience of French / German bilingualism in the Moselle and thinks it is 'just natural'. She also likes the English language and is very happy to see her elder child growing up to speak it so well. For the father 'it would have been absurd to speak to his own child in French' and anyway he 'had a rather "selfish" wish to establish an English "cell" around [him]self'.

The pattern in the family is as follows:

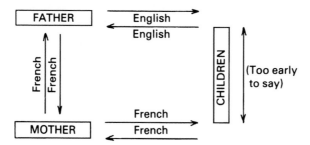

The father and mother converse in French, but the father always speaks to the children in English, whilst the mother always speaks to them in French. The mother understands English but very occasionally has difficulty in following when Carine and her father speak too quickly. This seems to bother husband more than wife though. She just shrugs and says: 'I can always ask them to repeat'. There is the 'odd bit of franglais, but when you work with scientists you're used to that'. Otherwise both parents are absolutely adamant that there have never been any problems: 'We don't know what all the fuss is about really'.

The father is very conscious of his role as 'source of English' in the family and admits to 'bombarding' his children with conversation, records and songs and rhymes. The two children seemed to start talking a little late, although the parents could no longer remember the exact details. Their development has so far followed almost exactly the same pattern: at first, they spoke French to both parents, with the father speaking to them in English. Carine only started speaking English with her father at the age of three years and nine months. He says: 'I can remember the particular train journey!' At the time of the study, Lydia, who is three, was still replying in French, although she clearly understood what was said to her in English. At a railway station in England recently she listened entranced to the loud-speaker and then reported to her father: 'English!'.

Carine, an open and lively child, was delighted to talk about her bilingualism and did so most articulately in English with a clear Yorkshire accent. She *loves* being bilingual, partly because she loves going to England and 'if I couldn't speak English, I couldn't speak to my cousins and friends there'. She finds it perfectly natural to talk English with her father, inside or outside the home: 'My daddy spoke to me in French once and *I felt all funny!*' She admits, though, that once when they were in England she did ask her mother to speak to her in English because strangers looked at them and it made her shy. When she makes friends she does not admit to being a bilingual immediately: 'I wait a bit, I don't sort of tell them everything. I might get turned off. I don't jump in straight away'. Asked what language she would do at school, she replied very firmly: '*Not* English!'. She reads and writes English well, but needs help with her spelling.

The whole family enjoys being bilingual, although perhaps it requires 'an extra effort' when the child is very small.

Case Study 2: Playing it by ear

Sinan and Arin are Turkish. Both studied English in Turkey from the moment they went to secondary school and for Sinan (the father) English was the only medium of instruction at school. English was also the medium of instruction at the university where they took their degrees. Ten years ago, they came to England to study at postgraduate level, and their son, Kerem, was born in Leeds. They have stayed in England since then and are both nearly balanced bilinguals. They always spoke Turkish together until their arrival in England. From that time on, they continued speaking Turkish but got used to switching to English frequently for social reasons.

The question of Kerem's bilingualism was not an issue originally, as they thought they were only going to stay in England for a little while. Arin spoke exclusively in Turkish to the baby for the first two years. Then Sinan got a five-year contract in England and Arin realised that Kerem might have difficulty if she sent him to an English nursery school. She then decided she should prepare Kerem and began to speak English to him just before he started nursery school. From that time on the parents kept speaking Turkish together in the home but addressed Kerem in English, and his ability to express himself in Turkish deteriorated. The presence of a Turkish nanny who spoke only Turkish to Kerem, from the time he was three until he was four-and-a-half, helped maintain his second language. However, he found communicating with her increasingly difficult and, taking advantage of the little English she was learning, he settled for a kind of pidgin when talking to her. Meanwhile, Kerem's English was developing perfectly normally through contact with his schoolmates. At that period the parents began to worry that Kerem might lose Turkish completely and find himself in trouble when the time came to go back to Turkey. This state of affairs, with Turkish definitely lagging behind Kerem's English, went on until Kerem was seven.

The situation changed dramatically when Arin took Kerem back to Turkey for a long summer holiday with the family. First of all, Arin had taken the trouble of preparing Kerem by speaking Turkish to him from time to time just before the trip. On arrival in Turkey, Kerem found it difficult to cope with the language but at the same time he found that his fluent English was a subject of admiration for his cousins. The realisation that his bilingualism made him different and was seen as an advantage by the others encouraged him in his learning of Turkish, and in two months his Turkish improved extremely quickly. He continued speaking Turkish at home with his parents after coming back but has now reverted to English, as before, except on certain occasions. Both Sinan and Arin still normally address Kerem in English. Arin thinks she switches to Turkish only in emotional situations, for instance if she is angry or in a hurry. Sinan probably switches more often. He finds that there are topics or words or even atmospheres that trigger the use of Turkish, but otherwise he has to make a conscious effort not to address Kerem in English. Kerem, on his part, rarely initiates exchanges in Turkish at home, except when there are Turkish visitors.

What is noticeable in this case is that although both parents were professional linguists they never tried to impose bilingualism on Kerem. Rather, in Arin's words, they 'did what seemed to be reasonable and best for Kerem given situations as they occurred'. In fact, both did worry that bilingualism might affect his intellectual development, but at the same time would have felt sorry (but not hurt, they insist) if Kerem had missed the opportunity of becoming bilingual and bicultural.

As for Kerem, although his English is clearly dominant, there is interference from Turkish in his pronunciation and he has an English accent in Turkish. However, since his long holiday in Turkey he has discovered for himself the advantages of being able to function as a full member of two linguistic communities. He's a good example of the fact that a child's own social life with his peer group determines the development of both his languages.

Fifteen years later:

Kerem (now working in the States) says:

> It's actually dawned on me that it's been a big struggle to BE in two languages . . . in that I think everyone strives to have one's identity, but in the English environment being bilingual is not recognised as having an identity unto itself, not yet at least and I am in the US as a Turkish Brit who wants to be American.

> I am immensely grateful to my parents for the flexible way in which they have handled my education. I would definitely bring up my family bilingually . . . because it does not restrict or limit one's mind to one point of view.

Case Study 3: Bilingualism begins at the front door

Ingrid is German and Jean François is French. They met in France during exchange visits between 'twinned' German and French towns. They now have three sons, Nicolas (8 yrs 1 mth), Matthias (4 yrs 11 mths) and Jerôme (2 yrs 10 mths). All of them are being brought up as bilinguals.

When they first met, Ingrid and Jean François spoke German together, since her French was not very good. When they married and set up home in France, though, they started speaking French, because she obviously needed it and that was clearly the best way of learning. This early switching has, it seems, left its mark on all subsequent arrangements. When the family goes to Germany, when parents and children are all together, they all speak German all the time, but when the children are alone with one another, they sometimes use French (see diagram 3). When they have German visitors at home, they also all speak German, and as Ingrid's mother spends two-and-a-half months per year with them, this is a considerable proportion of the time.

When they are alone at home the pattern is as in diagram 1. Jean François usually speaks French to the children and Ingrid usually speaks German. There are, however, important exceptions to this rule. The first is that Ingrid never speaks to the children in German outside the home when they are in France (see diagram 2). When she collects them from school, for example, they speak French as they walk along the pavement to their house, which is only 150 metres further along the same street, but as they enter the front door, everyone changes. So there is a strict 'geographical' division. Even so, should they be out of doors with someone monolingual German (such as their grandmother) the children will happily speak German with that person.

The second exception is that sometimes when the whole family is engaged in an activity together, they find they are all speaking German including Jean François. Ingrid says: 'It's an emotional thing. For example if I am baking with the children and Jean François is there, it feels better'. The same applies when they watch German television programmes together in France and 'whenever the atmosphere is specially relaxed'. In fact, Ingrid has tried to institutionalise this by ruling that when the family gathers for their midday meal they should all speak German. However, this has only been partially successful and Jean François admits that it is mostly his fault: 'Either I forget, and walk in and start talking French, or I'm just plain tired and can't be bothered'. It usually works for a few days at a time, though.

They find being bilingual 'completely natural, very, very useful and sometimes very amusing'. However, they admit that 'it could be a bit of an effort – for the parents, not the children'. In spite of this, they cannot imagine how they would manage if the family was not bilingual since, to take one example, the grandparents on each side are monolingual. They tell the story, laughing a lot, of Matthias at the age of two-and-a-half sitting solemnly between his two sets of grandparents 'translating' without any trace of difficulty or embarrassment. Bilingualism is both a cohesive force and 'an absolute necessity'.

They knew, from the beginning, that their family would have to be bilingual in some shape or form and they wanted 'at least to try to bring up the children speaking both languages well . . . even though there's always one

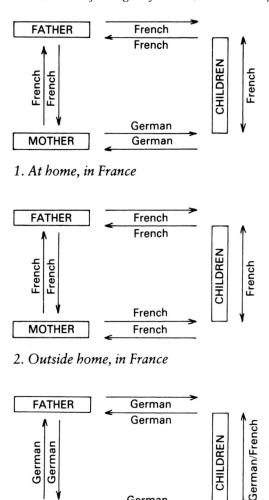

1. *At home, in France*

2. *Outside home, in France*

3. *In Germany*

that dominates. At the moment it's French, but after six months in Germany it would be German.' They took advice on the matter from paediatricians but 'found that opinions differed. One told us not to start on the second language until after the first was fully established. The other told us to go straight ahead with the two languages and that's what they us Ingrid 'just started speaking German whenever she was alone with Nicolas and that's how it's always been'. She reads bedtime stories in German and sings German songs and nursery rhymes.

The boys all speak both languages well, have no trouble at all switching from one language to another and never mix their languages, although they have all passed through an early phase when they did so. 'Sometimes they know a word in one language, usually French, and not in the other. Nicolas is rather careful in his choice of words, Matthias is much more spontaneous, and Jerôme is only just beginning.' The two older ones are not particularly shy about admitting they are bilingual, but absolutely refuse to 'put on a show' for anyone. Their parents find this perfectly understandable, and advise other parents never to insist on speaking the 'second' language to the child in front of his friends if the child objects.

At school, the two older boys are doing well. Nicolas has learnt to read and has transferred this skill to German with little difficulty. Until the age of six, he had a bedwetting problem, but their paediatrician assured them it had nothing to do with bilingualism and there hasn't been an 'accident' for two years now.

Matthias has been the source of some anxiety and embarrassment. As an experiment, German is being taught to the children at his nursery school – at first, he took this as a personal affront, an invasion of privacy and refused to have anything to do with the German 'classes'. Even when they sang songs and rhymes he already knew he refused – quite literally – to open his mouth. He then returned home to give imitations of his French teacher's German accent, of which he did not approve. However, that teacher has now won him round and he is beginning to rather enjoy helping her.

Above and beyond its practical uses, Jean François and Ingrid think that bilingualism is an intellectual asset: it 'widens their horizons. Even for a child of Matthias' age, just understanding that other people speak other languages and that there's nothing strange about it is a great advantage.'

Case Study 4: Conversational switching strategy

John, who is English, and Marie, who is a French-speaking Belgian, met in Germany about ten years ago, during an intensive summer course in German. John was working there after having completed a degree in Great Britain, while Marie taught in a domestic science school. Although they could speak each other's language – learnt at school – they spoke German together, as they were both keen to practise the language as much as possible. The couple then moved to the French-speaking part of Switzerland, where their first child, Roselyn, was born. The mother spoke French to the baby, while the father used English, but between themselves the parents always switched freely from English to French.

More recently, the family moved again and settled in London. Roselyn, who has acquired both languages without apparent difficulty, is now three-and-a-half. Normally she uses English with her father and French with her mother. However, when the three of them are together, she conforms to her parents' use of both languages, that is, it is the language chosen to open an exchange that determines the choice of language for the whole of this exchange. What is remarkable is the fact that the language chosen is not necessarily the dominant language of the parent who starts the exchange. John might very well initiate an exchange in French or Marie in English. Rather, it is the topic that determines the choice of language. Roselyn thus offers the extremely interesting example of a child who responds to a particular language rather than to a particular person and this does not seem to confuse her or to produce interference between the two languages. Although no systematic investigation has been made, it seems that this constant intra-family switching has made her particularly sensitive to perceptual factors as trigger mechanisms for choosing one or the other language. For example, her name is always pronounced *à la française* and if she is called by name from, say, another room, she will tend to reply in French even though the parent who called her may have expected the exchange to continue in English. The same pattern seems to apply to baby Etienne, Roselyn's little brother. Roselyn will address him in either language depending on the topic, although French tends to be dominant because the mother always addresses the baby in French.

In this family, both parents were very much aware of language problems and determined to try to bring up their children bilingually. Perhaps it is relevant here to remember that Marie comes from a linguistically and culturally divided country. The parents see themselves as 'linguistic bridges' between the children and the outside communities, and feel that speaking a particular language is more important than speaking like Mummy and Daddy. Both feel that parents have to be supportive and that correcting errors by means of repetition or expansion is useful. Lastly, it is worthwhile noticing that in spite of the extreme flexibility involved, the pattern of use for both languages is extremely consistent. This is no doubt the key to the success of this code-switching strategy.

Fifteen years later:

Etienne (now a student) writes:

> Having only one language or one culture would be like there was a big gap
> and by learning two languages from birth, your eyes are opened to the fact
> that there are other languages and cultures out there from a very young
> age. In my opinion, this can only benefit a child's development and curi-
> osity!

Case Study 5: Travelling light – bilingualism as basic baggage

Frédéric, who is French, is a top-flight commercial engineer who has spent
most of his life working several years at a time on major projects abroad.
His wife, Christine, is Austrian and they met through friends in Vienna.
Shortly after their marriage, they moved to Brazil where they stayed for five
years and where both their children, Antoine and Amélie, were born. At
the time they were interviewed, they had been back in France for ten
months and Antoine was three years, nine months old and his sister was
two years old. The family was due to leave again in four months' time, for
Chile, where they also expected to stay for a number of years.

Although neither Frédéric nor Christine was brought up bilingual, they
regarded bilingualism as an 'absolute necessity in our situation'. Neither
could imagine how on earth they would manage socially or professionally
if they didn't speak several languages. They both speak French, German,
Portuguese and English, and enjoy doing so. They are looking forward to
learning Spanish.

When Antoine was born, his parents assumed that he would grow up
bilingual in German and French and that he would learn Portuguese a
little later at playschool. Broadly speaking, this is what happened, but
there were a number of unforeseen developments. The first was that for
the first six months after her son was born, Christine found it very difficult
to speak to him *at all*: 'I had just got out of the habit of speaking German.
I speak French with my husband, I didn't want to speak French with the
baby but I couldn't get going in German either. It just seemed ridiculous to
be speaking German in Brazil to someone who couldn't understand a word
of what I was saying.' After about six months, she did bring herself to start
speaking regularly in German, though she still felt guilty about the delay.
With her second child, there was no such problem; she happily spoke to
her in German from the very beginning.

The next unexpected development was that when Antoine started speaking, it soon became clear that Portuguese was by far his best language. He spoke Portuguese with the maid at home and then started play-school at the age of two. He spoke French to both his parents, that is, he answered his mother's German in French. He also developed a 'private language' – an amazing and amusing hotch-potch of Portuguese, French and German which he loved to use at home.

When the family moved back to France, two things happened. The first was that Antoine, who was not quite three years old, simply forgot all his Portuguese, swiftly and completely, within a few months. The second was that he began speaking more and more French. Both parents were anxious because he continued 'to make lots of mistakes, though, even getting genders wrong sometimes'. Christine was considering dropping German, in case it was in some way the source of this problem. She was worried that 'it might be holding him back' and anyway he still refused to reply in German or even repeat what she said. They had no problems of any other kind with Antoine and no reason to believe that he was under some kind of strain: 'Perhaps he just doesn't have an ear for languages'.

What struck the visitor was how *well* Antoine spoke French, considering that he had only been in France for ten months. True, he made mistakes, for example, *je taime l'école*: as his father pointed out, he had invented the verb *taimer*. But he was relaxed, sociable and voluble, sitting chatting with a complete stranger while his parents arranged drinks. His parents, though, took a lot of persuading that his French was well up to scratch for a child of his age. (This judgement is impressionistic; no detailed observation or testing was possible.)

In fact, Antoine, like most children, seems to have unconsciously sorted out his linguistic priorities in a most efficient way. In Brazil, Portuguese was his best language because he used and needed it most, with French and German following – an order that also reflects the relative use and exposure to each language. Back in France, he dropped Portuguese completely because he no longer used or needed it and promoted French to first place. To start with, though, there was certainly a gap between his level of expression in Portuguese and French, and it is this 'backwardness' that was almost certainly the source of his parents' anxiety. Even if we accept that Antoine's development has not been problem-free (though the problems seem to be the parents', not his) it is quite clear that Antoine would have been worse off if he had come back to France unable to speak French.

The pattern in the family whilst they were in Brazil was:

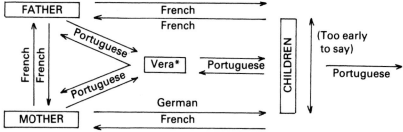

* Vera is the Portuguese-speaking maid.

In France, they simply dropped the Portuguese.

Case Study 6: Biculturalism, yes; bilingualism, no

Jane and Einar offer the interesting example of parents deciding *not* to bring up their children bilingually. Einar is Norwegian and he came to the UK to study civil engineering. His English was already extremely good and by the time he had finished his studies in Scotland, the few language difficulties he still had on arrival had been fully overcome. By that time, he had met Jane, who is English, and they had decided to settle in England after they got married. They always spoke English together and, although Jane started learning Norwegian after they had decided to get married, she says she could follow what was going on but could not carry out a discussion satisfactorily even after a six-month stay in Norway. In fact, with her parents-in-law, Jane got into the habit of speaking English while they addressed her in Norwegian.

Their children, Marianne and Erik, are now respectively fourteen and eleven years old. When Marianne was born, the mother naturally spoke English to the baby. Einar did not really decide not to speak Norwegian to his daughter, but simply found it perfectly natural to address her in English. Both feel that bilingualism in their home would have been superimposed and would have been a source of problems, partly because the mother could not speak Norwegian very well. Communication within the family would have been altered; for instance, there would have been innumerable occasions when Einar would have had to interpret what he had said to his daughter for his wife. Both feel that making such an effort simply for the sake of bringing up the children with two languages would have been a waste of time. Of course, if the mother had been the Norwegian speaker, and had felt the need of speaking her language to her children they would have approached the problem differently because she spent more time with the children, but in his case Einar never felt frustrated at all.

Another reason for their choice is the place of Norwegian amongst the languages of the world. Had the other language been a major European language like German or French, Einar might have felt differently about his children's education. But he felt that there was little advantage in their learning Norwegian. Indeed, the children never had any problems communicating with Norwegian people during their stays in Norway, since most people there can speak English. The only real problem they had was with their paternal grandfather, when he came to England to visit the family.

Einar's decision is not at all to be seen as the outcome of some sort of self-denial or rejection of his country of origin! If the limited usefulness of the Norwegian language is a fact that influenced the couple's decision against bilingualism in the home, Einar and Jane make all sorts of efforts to encourage and maintain the biculturalism of the children. There are translated Norwegian books around, records and so on. Each summer, the whole family goes to Norway for the holidays. There is no doubt that the whole family is very much aware of the Norwegian connection and enjoys it all.

It is also clear that in the event of one of the children expressing the wish to learn Norwegian, she or he would certainly not meet any opposition. Thus we have an example of a case where the 'loss' of one language happened naturally without preventing the maintenance of a strong link with the culture of the country where that language is spoken. This was possible not only because of the attachment of the parents to the Norwegian culture but also because of the status of English as an international language in that country.

Fifteen years later:

Erik (who is now working) says:

> 'I am proud of being 50% Viking, but embarrassed that I cannot speak the language, hence my taking of lessons. I just wish it was easier to learn' and 'I wish now that I was bilingual. Learning a language when young is much easier than when older. I wish more effort had been made to speak Norwegian in the home.'

Case Study 7: Family roots first – one parent, one language

Liisa and Jan are a Finnish couple living in Finland. She was brought up in a Finnish-speaking family while he came from a Swedish background. Liisa learnt Swedish at school, and describes herself as a fluent speaker of Swedish but admits to a strong preference for Finnish. In Jan's case, Finnish was learnt from a very early age. He studied medicine via the medium of both languages and is perfectly at ease in both.

The couple were determined to bring up their children with Finnish and Swedish for a variety of reasons. In the first place they wanted the children to be able to communicate with both sides of the family. Swedish would also be a means of access to other linguistic communities as well as to Scandinavian culture.

There were also social and work-related reasons for their decision: in most jobs, the knowledge of Swedish is a considerable advantage and, in all fields, Finnish cooperation with the rest of Scandinavia is increasing.

Thus, they saw their choice as a decision based on commonsense and from the start were favourable to the idea of bringing up their children as bilinguals. At the same time, they were very relaxed about it and had no dogmatic views on bilingualism. In particular, both were agreed that, since Liisa had more contact with the children, Finnish was very likely to be dominant. In fact, Liisa feels that a family needs roots and that in their case, 'home' is undoubtedly Finnish.

The two children, Anna and Jon, are now respectively five and three years old. Apart from special occasions when one of the languages is pre-ferred for social reasons, the parents consistently use their own language when addressing the children. They speak Finnish together and in family situations. The children speak Swedish with their father and with their grandmother with whom they have very frequent contact. They are also exposed to a lot of Swedish through radio and television. However, they do not have Swedish-speaking friends of their age and contact with their peer group is predominantly carried out in Finnish.

Anna went through periods when she mixed the two languages, but from the time she was four, she kept both languages completely separate and started reading in both of them. Jon, on the other hand, still shows signs of confusion and tends to speak Swedish by slotting Swedish words into Finnish constructions. Both are very much aware of the advantages of their bilingualism and fully enjoy ego-boosting roles like interpreting Swedish television programmes for their Finnish friends.

At the time Liisa was interviewed, the family was staying in England for a few months. As the father was away from home for most of the time and both children went to an English nursery school, the quality of their Swedish had seriously declined. However, at school, Anna did very well and acted as an interpreter for her brother who felt very frustrated when he was not able to do what he wanted because of his language difficulties.

It is worth noticing the way in which the mother's language influenced the pattern of bilingualism in the family, which is itself a picture of the bilingual situation to be found in Finland. The interesting consequence is that Swedish is the language 'at risk' when the children are confronted with the challenge of communicating with a peer group speaking a third language. However, it is remarkable to see how Anna, at five, coped with the situation. She managed to learn English extremely quickly for the purpose of immediate communication without getting confused, and at the same time, transferred the skill of interpreting from first-to-second language to first-to-third language for the benefit of her brother. This is yet another example of the extreme flexibility achieved by bilinguals.

This family's bilingual pattern is therefore:

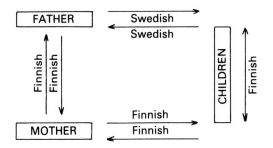

Case Study 8: My home is my (linguistic) castle

John and Kate arrived in France from their native England in 1968. They speak English with a marked Teesside accent, as indeed do all three of their children: Ellen, seventeen, John, sixteen, and Jenny, ten-and-a-half. The father is a French government research chemist, at present on secondment to the French brewing industry.

The parents do not consider themselves particularly gifted linguists: 'We learnt French the hard way'. Asked to elaborate, the father, who has the highest academic qualifications, adds with a touch of pride: 'I failed O-level French four times'.

The whole family has hung on tenaciously to its English identity. For the parents, there is no question of applying for French nationality despite considerable administrative pressure to do so and for the children there are frequent and greatly enjoyed holidays back in England.

Their linguistic arrangements are simple: English at home, French outside. Kate admits that when the children were smaller she went to some lengths to stop them speaking to one another in French. The only crack in this edifice is that the two elder children got into the habit of speaking French together at school because Ellen, in particular, did not like speaking English in front of her friends. Consequently, they some-times speak French to one another at home, when the parents are not present, although they both continue to speak English with their little sister. John still 'gets hot under the collar if anyone mixes the languages. I clamp down on it, it's sloppy'. In the interest of historical accuracy, it has to be mentioned that this statement was greeted with hoots of derision by the two teenagers, whose main objection was that their father was at least as guilty as they were, because of his passion for elaborate bilingual puns. However, this idiomatic and rapid-fire exchange was in itself enough to show any observer that they were capable of articulate expression of a high order in English and both parents agreed that 'when they wanted' the chil-dren were all completely successful at keeping the languages apart.

Their decision to establish and maintain a foreign home is not, they insist, a rejection of French. Both parents think that their children's bilingualism is 'wonderful' and accept that their children are 'mainly French'. They have also found it 'perfectly natural and for that reason can't really offer any advice'. They themselves did ask for advice at one point early on: an Italian lady warned them that their children risked 'brain fever' if exposed to two languages! However, they 'didn't really have any choice, and anyway in this family a bit of brain fever wouldn't really show!' The only problems they can recall are that Ellen became 'extremely conceited for a while about the fact that she could speak both languages' and that they find it difficult mixing English and French friends 'because you spend your whole time translating'.

Although the children learnt French at different ages (Ellen at the age of three, John at age one and Jenny simultaneously) there were no striking differences in the way they learnt or in the results. All three, according to their parents, 'speak English perfectly well, but French a little better'. They attribute this to their having a French education. All three are doing reas-onably well at school.

However, when asked whether they were a bit shy about being bilingual and what they thought about bilingualism, the children's answers did vary. Ellen never tells anyone at school, but none the less felt awkward when an

American girl joined her class, because she didn't know what language to use with her.

John, on the other hand, lets everybody know he is English (his parents accuse him of using it as an excuse for getting poor marks with teachers who do not realise he has spent almost his whole life in France). Jenny is shy about admitting it, but still insists that she likes being bilingual a lot.

The two elder children both read and write English. The family spent a year in the USA in 1978 and the schooling they received was enough to bring them up to scratch. Previously, John read very little in English, but since he discovered computers, he has become far more willing to do so.

As a visitor, you feel that their English roots go very deep, and when you hear Kate proclaiming half-seriously, 'Well, I'm not talking to any of *my* grandchildren in French!', you can't help speculating as to whether, in a couple of generations' time, there might not be a Teesside-English bilingual community thriving in Lorraine.

Case Study 9: 'Kids' lib' – accepting one's children's linguistic independence

Catherine is French. She had just started work teaching English in Paris when she met Paul, a Northern Irish research student, who was working on his thesis in French Literature at the Bibliothèque Nationale. For the first six months or so of their acquaintance, she spoke English to him while he spoke French to her. When she got a job as a translator in Sweden and he went back to university in England, they continued to use the same system for their correspondence. During the same period, Catherine became very fluent in English, which was the working language of the office where she was employed.

When they married and settled down in England, they developed a system whereby they would speak French during the week and English on Sundays. Although they lived in England, they spent at least four months every year in France, since Paul continued to take every opportunity he could to go to Paris to continue his research.

Three years later, they moved to the south of England. When their first son, Patrick, was born, their pattern of language use changed. French became the couple's language, Sundays included, and Catherine spoke only French to their child. The father only started speaking English to Patrick once it was clear that his French was well-grounded. Patrick was about eighteen months old at this time.

This was followed by an interesting period during which Patrick developed a sex-based theory of language choice: you spoke French to women and English to men. To his great surprise, the theory collapsed when he travelled to France with his parents and found that neither his grandfather nor his uncle spoke English!

At the age of three, Patrick had to go to an English nursery school while his mother was in hospital. He found this experience very distressing, although it is not clear whether it was his mother's sudden absence, the impending birth of a brother or being suddenly plunged into a group of English-speaking children which caused this.

When the second child, Michael, was about fifteen months old, the family spent a year in Canada. For about three months after their return to England, the children would use English at school, switching to French when they came back home. Then, within the space of a single week, they stopped using French when they played together and started using English instead. They kept French as a private language, to be used only with their mother.

Since then, the following pattern has been firmly established: the parents speak French together and the mother addresses her sons in French, but they reply in English. Their father addresses them in English, except when the mother is present, in which case he uses French. The boys always reply in English. This pattern can be diagrammed as follows:

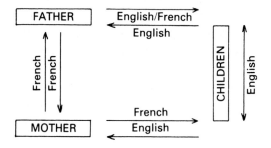

At the time of interviewing, Patrick and Michael were sixteen and thirteen years old respectively. They both understood French perfectly well and spoke it with a good accent. Their frequent trips to France had certainly helped maintain their oral proficiency. Their mother considered that 'as a rule their French vocabulary was relatively small and their use of French syntax limited to simple sentences'. Moreover, apart from French comics like *Pif* or *Tintin*, and the occasional specialised interest magazine (electronics, etc.) they did not usually read French. When writing, their spelling mistakes were usually 'phonetic'. However, these weaknesses have proved to be only a passing problem, since work on written French at school has improved their performances considerably. Since then, they have both got A grades at O-level French, but being scientists they dropped French at A-level.

Patrick and Michael's case is interesting because of the way in which they took their linguistic independence early on, only maintaining French in order to understand their mother. They seem to have operated on the basis of two principles: first, that the individual members of a family have the right to express themselves in the language of their choice and, secondly, the principle of least effort. There is no way of knowing, of course, what the relative importance of these two principles was. However, there was a clear family consensus: their father had chosen to speak French because of his special interest in that language and their mother because it was her preferred means of expression. They could drop speaking French if they so wished: all that was necessary for efficient communication within the family was that they should understand French – which they did. In this way, each member of the family, parents and children alike, was able to speak the language which he or she preferred.

The children's behaviour seems to reveal a very sensible attitude towards language choice and the parents were probably wise to let it develop as it did; any resistance on their part would almost certainly only have resulted in friction. By recognising that the children's social life and their activities with their peer group determined their preference for English, but at the same time maintaining their own use of French at home, the parents made it possible for the children to live in constant contact with the French language and culture without forcing it on them. Should the occasion arise, it is clear that either boy could rapidly become perfectly fluent in French, and with only a minimum of effort. Their mother feels that she has given them the basis of the language and that, if they need French in their professional lives, they will be able to make use of that knowledge.

Case Study 10: Traces from childhood

Eva is Swedish and has lived in England for thirteen years. She studied English and French at university in Sweden and, although Swedish is her dominant language, she feels more at ease in English when talking about certain topics, or when facing certain delicate social situations. Swedish is the language to which she feels emotionally attached because it is the language of her youth. She goes back to Sweden nearly every year but the pattern of social interchange has changed since she left and she feels socially insecure when using, for instance, an address system different from the one she was accustomed to.

She met her English husband in Sweden fifteen years ago. Richard – now a freelance translator – was brought up in an English-speaking home and studied German and French for his degree. He started learning Swedish by going to evening classes and went to Sweden for three months. When they first met, Eva and Richard spoke French together; afterwards they spoke Swedish consistently. Richard's Swedish pronunciation is excellent and people cannot tell he is not Swedish. However, Eva would not describe him as a balanced bilingual. His 'passive' vocabulary is not very extensive in Swedish and his ability to 'guess' the meaning of words in the speech of Norwegian or Danish people is not as developed as that of a Swedish native-speaker.

When their son, Peter, was born, they had settled in England and they decided to bring up the child bilingually. During the first two years, both parents spoke Swedish to the child although Richard read stories to Peter in English. Then the family went to Holland for two years. Eva looked after the child and continued speaking Swedish to him. He went to a local play-group where there were English-speaking children and, after a phase during which he tried to impose Swedish on the others, started to learn English. Although Swedish was still dominant, he could easily express himself in English by the time they came back to England. From the moment he started going first to a playgroup, then to school in England, his English developed quickly. After a few months, Eva realised that the school teacher did not even know Peter had another language, and was delighted. Eva thinks that by the time he was six, Peter was a balanced bilingual, but always associated each language with particular situations rather than particular individuals, that is, he tended to speak Swedish in Sweden during the holidays and English in England.

At home, the situation developed very quickly. Peter started speaking English to his parents during the first year he was at school. When he did so, they would reply in Swedish but gradually he lost the habit of express-ing himself in Swedish and now seems to be embarrassed when doing so – although he addresses the dogs in Swedish. Swedish in fact has become the parents' private language. The way language choice operates when the three are together is very revealing in that respect. If Eva speaks to Richard in Swedish, then thinks Peter would find what she has to say interesting, she calls for Peter's attention and switches to English. By systematically switching to English when they want Peter to be included, the parents implicitly state that he is not to be involved when conversation goes on in Swedish. In fact, Eva believes Peter can follow conversations much better than he lets on. Peter is now twelve and the parents think that the best solution for helping Peter would be to make him spend more time in Sweden in an environment where he would have to communicate in Swedish independently from them.

They think Peter is uncooperative about speaking Swedish in England mostly because Swedish is not necessary, but also because of the way he speaks Swedish, which Eva describes as characteristically 'childish'. The syntax and vocabulary available to him no longer match the communicative needs of his age – which is not very surprising since he has not used Swedish for a very long time – and his pronunciation and voice quality (very high pitched and 'wailing') are definitely those of a small child. He seems to need to resume the personality of the child he was when he could speak Swedish fluently in order to get it right. Obviously, now that he is an adolescent, there is a growing tension between his present self – which he can only express in English – and the child he used to be. This kind of crystallisation of a past mode of speaking which is no longer adapted to his present communicative needs is a cause of embarrassment for Peter, and all the more so because he is particularly good in English and is well above average as regards syntax and vocabulary. What is remarkable too is that this 'childish' language variety has resisted the influence of his parents' Swedish on the one hand and interference from English on the other for about six years.

It is interesting to compare this case with Case Studies 9 and 12. In Case Study 12, the maintenance of the 'second' language is easily achieved by regular and prolonged visits to Spain where Joanna has good friends. In Case Study 9 the same pattern seems to have developed, but the presence of two children has helped resolve the conflict by maintaining the balance between parents and children in terms of number, thus multiplying the number of possible communicative networks in the family and avoiding the problem of isolation apparent in Peter's case. It is very likely that his personal involvement with a Swedish peer group within the next few years will be the key to his weaker language developing into his second adult language.

Fifteen years later:

Peter's experience of bilingualism as an adult is consistent with the pattern of his development as an adolescent. He lives in the UK and, now thirty-three years old, he says:

> I don't really make much use of my Swedish, mostly because I don't get the
> opportunity. When I have met (for example) Swedish business colleagues
> I have found it helpful and rather fun to speak to them in their own lan-
> guage. Unfortunately this happens all too infrequently.

He feels this dependency on others in order to speak and maintain his proficiency in Swedish may also reflect the fact that his literacy remains unde-
veloped:

> I feel that my spoken and written English is very good. However, my
> Swedish is deteriorating. I was never taught to read or write in Swedish
> (which was a shame looking back), so I would find it difficult to study the
> language on my own.

Case Study 11: A cultural heritage – one parent, one language

Martine and Ronald met in 1970 in one of the vineyards bordering the river
Herault where they were both working as grape-pickers. She (Martine) is
French and he (Ronald) is American. At the time they met, her English was
not very advanced; she did a degree in classics. Ronald studied engineering in Paris for three years and so learnt French for essentially communicative as well as academic purposes.

French has always been their common language and, from the beginning, Martine has got into the habit of correcting Ronald systematically
whenever he makes a mistake. At the time of interviewing, they had lived
in England for eight years. Martine works full-time in a bookshop and feels
perfectly at ease in English. There are even certain topics that she finds
difficult to discuss in French. Ronald has not reached the same level of
competence in his second language. In spite of the fact that he speaks it
fluently, his accent is still very strong and there are times when he finds it
difficult to express complex ideas in French.

There are two children in the family: Anne, aged five and Dominic, aged
three. Normally, the children speak English together and to their friends at
school. They have had far more contact with English-speaking children
than with French-speaking ones because they both went to an English
nursery school from the age of fourteen months. The only occasion when
they spontaneously choose to use French together is when they sing songs
in the evenings.

Martine always addresses the children in French and is the one that, as
a rule, they identify with the language: if she listens to the radio, it will be
a French station. Moreover, she reads a lot, and so French books are left

lying all around the house. The one occasion when she does not speak French in the family is when Ronald's mother visits them.

Ronald is similarly consistent in his use of English with the children. Again, the only exception is that he speaks French to them when the family is on holiday at their grandparents' in France. Maintaining the relationship between the French grandparents and the children was an important factor in the parents' desire to have bilingual children.

Without being overly rigid about it, they operate on the 'one parent, one language' principle. The only breach in this 'code of conduct' (other than the two situations already mentioned) occurs at bedtime: the children choose a story in a book and the mother and father take it in turns to read. So it is the book that determines the choice of language, not the reader.

Although Anne is dominant in English – her 'first words' were in English – there are times when she seems genuinely 'balanced', usually in the weeks following a trip to France when she has just started using English again and French has not yet receded. (This is a well-known and frequently reported phenomenon in children brought up with this pattern of use.) She has already stayed on her own with her grandparents for periods of up to six weeks at a time, and each time she returns home she speaks only French for a week or so, even with her father. She is beginning to read in English and showing an interest in written French too.

Anne was rather late in her speech development and Martine and Ronald thought it might be associated with the two languages. At school, there were problems at one stage: people did not understand what she was saying in English and meanwhile she developed an English accent when she spoke French. However, as she was clearly one of the best pupils in her class academically, they did not worry unduly and the problems proved to be temporary.

Dominic started speaking at an earlier age than Anne, but in other ways seems to be a later developer. He has not, however, had any of his sister's problems. The parents think that this may very well be because they monitor his speech less carefully than Anne's.

Although Martine and Ronald wanted their children to speak both languages, they adopted a very relaxed attitude about it. In particular, they were ready to accept that it might not work: they had friends who had used the 'one parent, one language' principle and had succeeded, but another couple they knew had tried the same principle and failed. They could only try and hope it would work. Their expectations in bringing up the children with two languages are manifold, but their overall aim is to help the children maintain the dual language identity that characterises their parents:

it is 'some sort of heritage rather than an investment!'. Martine would like to see their children keep on speaking French and later on reading French literature for pleasure. There are also practical aspects to consider. It may be wise to keep open the option of moving to / living in / studying in France. By and large, bilingualism is an advantage. Apart from the purely 'linguistic' achievement, the children's cross-cultural life – living essentially *à la française* in an English environment – should help the children to become tolerant and flexible or, as their mother puts it, 'more human'.

Fifteen years later:

Anne (now a student) writes:

> I would definitely bring up my children bilingually. It offers children a much broader and interesting understanding of the world, lessens their tendency to generalise on the basis of their own surroundings and makes them more tolerant to 'otherness', as well as helps them learn other languages.

Dominic (now working) writes:

> I can't imagine what it would be like to have only one language. A lot of my friends are of one culture and I see them within it but cannot imagine myself in a different situation' . . . The thing which annoys me most is not being able to communicate with my cousins as well as I would like. As they are of my generation, they speak French with as many slang words as they can fit in . . . when I join the conversation I cannot use the same language and so I sound very basic.

Case Study 12: Two homes, two languages, two cultures

Teresa is Spanish and started learning English at the age of 22, when she came to a language school in England. She obtained the Cambridge First Certificate within nine months and went on later to pass the Cambridge Certificate of Proficiency examination. By that time she had been offered a job as an interpreter in a local firm and had met her husband, who is English. Now that she has lived in England for over ten years, she feels that she is totally bilingual. There are even domains where English is her preferred language.

Her husband, John, had a very different linguistic background. His own family had a 'French connection' on his mother's side, which had made him familiar with French language and culture from an early age, but although he achieved a good command of oral French he says he never really felt bilingual. The task of learning Spanish at 23 was 'an immense struggle' for him and he found that it obliterated most of the French he knew. However, he can follow most conversations, can manage on the phone and has no difficulty surviving in Spanish-speaking countries when he has to do so for business purposes or during holidays. When it comes to complex business discussions, though, he feels that his command of the language is inadequate. He also finds holidays in Spain with his wife's family frustrating, because he cannot integrate and finds himself excluded from a good many conversations. The couple always use English together except in the presence of Spanish friends in Spain.

Their daughter Joanna is now eleven. The parents did not discuss the question of the child's potential bilingualism before she was born and they say they were completely opportunistic about it. Instead of formulating rules as to who would talk what, they took the relaxed view that what felt 'natural' to them and elicited a good response from the child must be right. At the very beginning, Teresa talked Spanish to the baby and John often did too. Although Spanish was therefore dominant, Joanna was also acquiring English at the same time, first from her English nanny and then at the day nursery she attended. At about the time Joanna started school, her mother began speaking English to her, reserving Spanish for intimate or emotional situations.

From that time on, Joanna lived in an essentially English-speaking home in England. However, every summer her mother takes her to Spain for a three-month holiday, during which they speak exclusively Spanish in the family context.

Joanna seems to switch automatically from one language to another without difficulty and is perfectly at ease with this 'two homes, two languages, two cultures' pattern. She has Spanish friends in Spain and English friends in England and moves happily from one world to the other. Although there are a number of activities that she does carry out in Spanish with her mother when they are in England, she seems to prefer to keep these two worlds separate. She does not like her mother to speak Spanish with her in front of her English friends and in general shows quite clearly that, as far as she is concerned, Spanish is just 'not on' in England.

At the present stage in her linguistic development, her Spanish does not seem to be advancing at the same rate as her English. In particular, her schooling in England is helping her develop an increasingly wide range of verbal skills and there is some interference from English in her Spanish. Her parents feel that they might try to reinforce her weaker language by encouraging her to read more in Spanish. If Joanna is given the opportunity of learning new things through the medium of Spanish, it is less likely that it will just remain 'the language one speaks in the holidays' for her.

Joanna is an interesting example of successful bilingual development. She has operated on the principle of 'one country, one language' rather than on the frequently advocated 'one parent, one language'. This shows that it is not necessary for a child to have a bilingual home in order to become bilingual: one can just as well have two monolingual homes. Of course, this is by no means an option which is available to everyone, but where such a choice does exist it seems to work well. The only drawback is that sometimes, as families get bigger and time passes, contacts become less frequent and the second language tails off imperceptibly. In Joanna's case, her mother's lasting attachment to her country of origin over the years was a crucial factor in her acquisition of Spanish. So, too, was her father's willing acceptance of the Spanish side of the family (after all, he could have insisted on holidays elsewhere). Once again, we can see how influential the parents' attitude towards the 'second' language can be.

Case Study 13: Easy come, easy go

Maria and Roger belong to the growing number of families who move from country to country because of the father's job. At the time of the interview, they had just moved back to England – Roger's country – after a seven-year period during which they had been in Austria for two years, returned to England for a few months, then left again for Mexico for four years. Their two children, Helena, nine, and Philip, seven, had therefore been faced with the problem of coping with a succession of new languages, new homes and new friends.

The linguistic make-up of the family was made more complex by the fact that the mother's native language was not English. Maria was brought up in Romania, where she studied several languages, including Russian and French, at school. She learnt English on her own with 'teach yourself' books and conversation classes. In 1969 she came to England and worked in a laboratory. She met Roger in England. Helena was born and for the first two years or so the pattern of bilingualism within the family was as shown below. Helena, of course, was only just beginning to speak towards

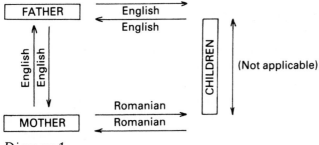

Diagram 1

the end of the period in question. Philip was born just before the family left for Austria.

When it came to moving to Austria, the parents decided that having two languages was enough and that it would be better for the children to have only one 'home language'. English was the language chosen, and the mother spoke English to Philip from the very start. She also stopped speaking Romanian to Helena, which did not seem to worry Helena at all. Helena and Philip always spoke English together.

In Austria, then, only English was spoken in the home, but apart from the baby, the whole family learnt German. At this point, the pattern of bilingualism was that of a monolingual family within a foreign community:

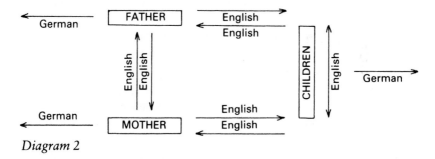

Diagram 2

Maria, who had no German at all on arrival, went to evening classes. Roger, who says that his knowledge of German was already 'reasonable' and was sufficient for his working life, improved his overall proficiency by daily contact with the language. Helena, who was two years old when she arrived in Austria, started kindergarten at the age of three: it took her about six months to cope with the new situation and the period of adaptation was not a particularly easy one, since she refused to sleep at school, which meant that she got very tired. She never used German at home and outside school she played only with English friends.

By the time the family left Austria and came back to England, Helena was four and her brother two. Her parents say that at school in England Helena did well, but only relatively so; she made considerable progress, but because her English was not as good as the other children's, she did not catch up in the short time available. She was at the school for only a term before she left again, for Mexico. By this time, she had forgotten German.

Philip, who was always a very quiet child, did not speak very much before the age of two-and-a-half. In England he went to a nursery school. During their four-year stay in Mexico, the family's home language was English throughout. In other words diagram 2 still applies, although with Spanish instead of German, of course. This time, though, the outside language had more impact on the children: they both learnt Spanish.

Helena went to an English school, where the teachers were English but where 90 per cent of the children were Spanish speakers and used Spanish amongst themselves. It took her between six months and a year to learn the new language. Helena came back to England a year before the rest of the family and went to boarding school. When she rejoined the family in Mexico for a holiday after two terms, she had apparently forgotten all her Spanish and was unable to say a word, but it all came back to her during her two-month stay.

Philip, who was nearly three when he arrived in Mexico, went to a Spanish-speaking school at first, but refused to speak Spanish. He was then transferred to his sister's school and learnt Spanish in about six months both from friends at school and from the Mexican maid at home.

Now that the family has been back in England for nine months, the parents say Helena still speaks Spanish well, but she does not try to keep it up: she does not read anything in Spanish, nor can she write it properly. She has chosen French as her foreign language at school because she did not enjoy Spanish at school in Mexico. Twenty-one months after her return, Helena's English is still somewhat limited in terms of vocabulary and fluency, and her parents also think she is a rather slow reader. On the other hand, she has a good accent and intonation and her father says she is very pleasant to listen to. At school (she is no longer at boarding school) her results are good – no more, no less: there is no evidence that her life abroad has had any deleterious effect on her academic ability.

Philip seemed to offer a more balanced pattern of bilingualism when he came back to England: his English was clearly dominant as far as reading and writing were concerned, but his oral Spanish was very good. None the less, there was some Spanish interference in his English as regards stress and intonation (his parents think this might have been due to his mother's accent). At the time of the interview, his spoken Spanish was becoming less 'automatic' and he was obviously in the process of forgetting the language. Like his sister, he had decided to take French as his first foreign language at school the following year.

The family's frequent moves have had important consequences for the patterns of language use within the family. The most important of these was the replacement of the 'natural' bilingualism internal to the family (that is, Romanian / English) by a succession of 'external' types of bilingualism (English / German, English / Spanish) resulting from the contact with outside communities. This major change was due to the parents' feeling 'that in our circumstances, it was better for the children to have only one home language': in their eyes the advantage of this move was that it reinforced family unity, but this was done at the expense of the mother's language and led to the loss of bilingual communication within the home.

Maria and Roger were not particularly determined to bring up their children bilingually, but nor did they see any reason why the children should not learn other languages when they had the chance. Moreover, they did not find that the alternatives available were either attractive, since they all involved some kind of split in the family, such as different members speaking different pairs of languages, or practical (since their base was in England). Having only one home language was aimed at ensuring that the children would feel that they had roots in England, that however much they travelled, they were part of the English community. Moreover, without being in any sense opposed to bilingualism, they did not wish to make life unnecessarily complicated for their children. Lastly, their decision was in keeping with their feeling that 'not concentrating on only one language might be damaging' for the children's language development.

A further result of their adoption of English as the only home language while abroad was that it led the father to be very conscious of his role as the only reliable norm of reference for that language. He deliberately got into the habit of speaking in a clear, slow, precise way, using only Standard English and carefully avoiding slang.

Because their main concern was to ensure a good grounding in at least one language, the parents are not at all bothered about the fact that their children are forgetting the languages they learnt abroad. Nor do they regret that neither of them seemed to take a liking to Spanish or German. They were always confident in the children's 'toughness' and learning to cope with people who speak other languages is just a fact of life. It may have been hard on the children at times, but it was hard on them, too! At the time of interviewing, they were in fact a monolingual family composed of individuals who had all had the experience of functioning in at least two languages. For them, bilingualism was a temporary measure necessary in the short term for purely practical reasons and in the long term to maintain a 'home base' language properly.

Case Study 14: Determination – and a sense of humour

I spotted Birgitte and Nigel on the Danish ferry sailing from Esbjerg to Harwich. There were two children of about ten years old, a boy and a girl, and they both seemed to use English and Danish to address either of their parents in an apparently random manner. A week later, when I interviewed the parents, I was told that the pattern of switching I had observed was indeed random and occurred only in 'boat situations': the family normally functions in English at home in England, the father's country, and in Danish in Denmark when they visit the mother's family. Only when they are actually in transit between the two countries is this pattern disturbed.

Birgitte was brought up in Denmark and took German as her first foreign language when she started at secondary school. The following year, she also began learning English, but her German became far more proficient thanks to frequent contacts with a German penfriend. She went to England for the first time at the age of eighteen, working on the domestic staff of an Esso Research and Development Centre. During this time, her English improved dramatically, and she also met her future husband, who was training as a chemist.

She returned to Denmark to take a three-year course in organisation methods, with Nigel coming over each summer. They always spoke to one another in English, but he still 'picked up a few words for everyday survival' as well as learning 'polite things to say in company'. In 1967 they got married (the carefully rehearsed speech he made in Danish at their wedding was a landmark in his acquisition of Danish) and they settled in England.

Birgitte admits that she missed her family and the Danish way of life at the beginning, but she managed to make her home *hyggelig* ('cosy') enough to feel happy. For the first four years they were both working and so they could afford to go to Denmark at least once a year. Moreover, frequent visits from various members of her side of the family meant that she never felt cut off from her roots in Denmark. Indeed, the attraction of Denmark was very strong for both of them and since Nigel was dissatisfied with his job in England, they seriously considered moving to Denmark, although in the end this project did not come off.

When they started their family, they talked about the language problem and decided they wanted to bring up their children bilingually, although they did not know exactly how they were going to do it. A particular incident they witnessed served to stiffen their resolve: the six-year-old daughter of Danish relatives who had moved to Canada with her parents had been brought up speaking only English. When she came back to visit her grandparents, she could not talk with them. Birgitte and Nigel saw that it was very distressing for the grandparents not to be able to communicate with the child or to build up any kind of close relationship and they determined to avoid making the same mistake.

When their daughter Lisa was born, the mother spoke to her mainly in English, although Danish frequently cropped up in the form of lullabies, rhymes and songs. When Lisa started talking, she spoke English, but could understand Danish without any difficulty. Her Danish grandmother came on frequent visits and, when she did, Danish was spoken at home. There were also regular trips to Denmark, and this meant that alltogether Lisa spent lengthy periods in a Danish-speaking environment. Usually, when she arrived in Denmark she would continue speaking English for two or three weeks, and then switch to Danish. She never seemed to mix the two languages.

Lisa's brother Ian at first put up far more resistance to learning Danish. His father recalls an occasion when Ian was three years old and they had just arrived in Denmark. They were met by members of the family, including a Danish cousin of the same age. In the car, the two children had a long conversation, each using his own language, and they obviously understood one another perfectly well. The adults were so fascinated by what was going on in the back of the car that they nearly had an accident.

Ian continued to avoid actually speaking the language until he was about five years old. The parents believe that they may have given him less encouragement than his sister: because they were anxious to be 'good parents' they feel they exercised far more control over their daughter than they did over their son. They simply let him develop at his own pace, waiting for the day when he would be personally motivated to speak Danish. This came during a seaside holiday when he was about six. He met some children on the beach and he started playing with them, and talking Danish at the same time.

The children are now twelve and nine years old. Lisa is perfectly fluent in Danish. Her mother says that very occasionally she will get a word stress wrong, but normally she passes for a native-speaker. She reads Danish without difficulty, but prefers English books. She does have problems writing, though, and definitely needs help. Until recently, she was always happy about being bilingual, but now she has entered a new phase: she does not like to be different from her friends and is upset if her mother addresses her in Danish in front of them.

Ian has not reached this difficult stage yet. He can now speak fluent Danish and is perfectly happy to be seen using two languages. When his Danish cousin came to England and went to school with him he was very proud to interpret for him in class, and when the village children played with them in the garden, it sounded as if the Vikings had invaded again! His reading ability in Danish is difficult to assess since he reads, but only short, easy books.

Both children listen to a lot of Danish on tape and spend hours listening to Danish cassettes and records. They have no difficulty at all understanding radio programmes in Danish. They are now old enough to realise that their father's Danish is approximative and that he does not seem to be able to get rid of a number of deep-seated deficiencies. He himself says that he can make himself understood in simple matters, but actually translates from English to Danish when he is talking. He can read and understand the gist of a newspaper article but probably misses out on many details. As for listening, the news on the radio is too fast; however, when the content is predictable he can manage even difficult tasks such as arranging appointments on the telephone.

Birgitte has never worried about her husband speaking his limited Danish to the children, as he does when they are in a Danish family context; she assumes that they have enough contact with standard Danish otherwise. When he speaks Danish in company, Nigel is often confronted with his children's 'raised eyebrows' as well as with 'comments from the side of the mouth so that no one else can hear, to the effect that "that wasn't right, Dad!"'. He says, however, that he has never felt that he should have made the effort of speaking Danish correctly for the children's sake. He has acquired enough Danish for his purposes and although he gets frustrated when he gets 'stuck' in Denmark, he doesn't believe that his own level of Danish has made any difference to the children's linguistic development.

Rather, both parents believe that what counts is one's determination and desire to maintain both languages in the home – something which requires a lot of effort from *everybody* in the family. They all have to make allowances for the bilingual situation. They have seen many examples of couples in their situation who gave up using Danish at home. Either the father would not make the effort of learning some Danish or he would actually forbid the mother to speak her language to the children, usually on the grounds that Danish was not a 'useful' language. Birgitte and Nigel think that the 'usefulness' argument is a misguided one; a parent should never prevent a child from building close relationships with people who love them, whatever the language concerned, as it is essential for their cognitive and emotional development.

Case Study 15: Language as religious and social identity

Naima and Elhadj arrived in France in 1974, shortly after their marriage, and all three of their children – Wided (eight-and-a-half), Cihame (six) and Sophian (three-and-a-half) were born there. Naima is Moroccan and her husband Algerian. Given the unhappy state of the relationship between those two countries, this has given them quite a few headaches in the past. For much of the period in question they could not return as a couple to either country to visit their families.

Despite this – or is it because of it? – they are both deeply committed to the ideal of Arab unity. To the extent that it is possible to distinguish between the two, their commitment is far more religious and cultural than political. Both are religious and Naima unhesitatingly gave religion as their main reason for bringing up the children bilingually: 'They must read the Koran'. Very closely related to this, though, is the feeling that not to speak Arabic would involve a loss of social identity: 'You have to speak Arabic to be your true self'. Two other reasons were also given which, although not as fundamental, were of clear practical importance: to be able to speak with their relatives when they go home, which they do about once a year, and to be prepared for resettlement in Algeria, should the government recall Elhadj.

With one exception, their experience of bilingualism has been very positive. They did not set out with any preconceived ideas since both of them

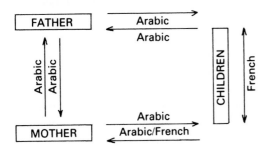

were monolingual in Arabic, but once in France they knew that they had no practical choice, and anyway they had plenty of Arabic-speaking friends and colleagues who had all brought up their children bilingually without any particular difficulty. The advice they received from these people was to speak Arabic at home, and to talk with the children as often as possible. By and large, they have followed this advice and the results are satisfactory.

The only problem came when Wided used some Arabic at school one day and immediately found herself the subject of racist remarks by another child her own age. Puzzled and upset, she returned home to tell her mother: 'Mummy, I don't want to speak Arabic any more'. As a result, Naima, who was herself very shocked, was less strict on insisting on Arabic at home. She now feels this was a great mistake, for a number of reasons. Wided soon got over her unpleasant experience, but the 'damage' was done – the children knew they could speak to her in French, and began speaking French amongst themselves. Their father, though, still applies the rules and if one of the children speaks to him in French, he simply pretends that he has not heard, or that he has not understood what they said. They often have Arabic-speaking friends visit them at home, at which time no French at all is spoken.

All three children are bilingual, but not to the same degree. Wided, who seemed to pick up French the most easily and quickly of the three, none the less has a slight accent. She is just starting on written Arabic. The last time they returned to Morocco, Wided seemed to forget every word of French in a very short time, but it all came back just as quickly. Cihame did much the same, but less dramatically. Both girls are interested in their bilingualism and talk about it with their mother: all three insist that it is 'very great fun'. They never try to hide their bilingualism; they have been taught by their parents to be proud of being Arabs. They do mix French words with their Arabic sometimes, but never put any Arabic words in with their French. The girls are doing well at school. They are already doing some German and seem to show considerable talent for it.

At three-and-a-half, their little brother Sophian is as lively and talkative as his elder sisters. For the moment, his mother says, it is quite impossible to say which of his languages is best, but of course she expects it to be French soon (he has just started nursery school). This does not worry her at all. Now that she has seen how well the girls manage, even if their French is not perfect, she is confident that all will go well.

It would be difficult to find a clearer example of the way in which a positive attitude towards the languages concerned forms successful bilingualism. The pride and respect that Naima and Elhadj have for their language and culture are clearly being passed on to their children. This is particularly striking in view of the linguistic difficulties experienced by a large proportion of France's North African community.

Case Study 16: Bilingualism – and a better life

Elsewhere in this book, we discuss the distinction between 'folk' and 'elitist' bilingualism. 'Folk' bilingualism is the term used to describe bilingualism resulting from mass immigration and historical change, whilst 'elitist' or as we argue 'elective' bilingualism is much more individual, varied and sporadic. This distinction, although useful, is an over-simplification, as the case study described here shows. In the space of one generation, Luisa and Pablo's family have made the transition from one category to the other. They provide an example of social mobility in which bilingualism has played an important role.

When Pablo arrived in France from Spain in 1964, he was an immigrant, illiterate in Spanish, who did not speak a word of French. The emigration service only gave him a month's notice of which country he was going to, so there was no question of preparing himself before his departure. During his early days in France he had to use gestures to make himself understood. He found learning French a slow and difficult business, only picking up a little at work in the steel mills and in the street. Indeed, it was only later, when his wife joined him the following year, that he began to make progress by listening to his two elder children (boys aged seven and three-and-a-half at the time) learning the language themselves. He now speaks, reads and understands both languages fluently. His written Spanish is also good, but he feels that his written French is shaky.

At home, Pablo and Luisa have always spoken Spanish together, and with their children. This is almost certainly why Luisa even now speaks and reads only a little French, since, as a housewife, she had no exposure to that language. She finds it difficult to handle a second language and is amazed, and proud, to see how well her children have managed. She is distressed to see that Sebastian, her eldest son who has a French wife, is bringing up his children speaking only French, and admits to nagging him about it. He, however, is a skilled technician with no intention of going back to Spain and so cannot see the point. He was the only one of the five children to receive any formal instruction in Spanish, since his father, on the advice of a friend, enrolled him in a correspondence course even before he arrived in France.

Contacts with Spain have been kept up by a number of other means: the radio, a monthly magazine, neighbours, but most important of all, an annual holiday. None of the children has any problems speaking with their relatives and their mother 'feels very Spanish'. Only Pablo had any reservations because Spanish relatives pull his leg and call him 'the Frenchman', although he doesn't feel French at all. None the less, both parents agree that, even if bilingualism might not be absolutely necessary, it is still a good thing to know two different cultures and to be able to make yourself understood in two different countries.

The three children born in France learnt Spanish at home and each of them only started French at about four years old, when they went to nursery school. However, all the children speak French to one another, even at home. At primary and secondary school, their bilingualism was never discussed and they doubt if their teachers were even aware of it. José, the second son, is now at university, and will probably be followed by Francisco, who has just got his 'Bac', and Manuel. Their sister, Trinidad who is eighteen, has not yet decided what she is going to do.

Asked how they felt themselves about being bilinguals, the four younger children replied *Bof* (a French expression meaning that there really isn't much to say) and they then went on to discuss it in great detail. It was generally agreed that Francisco and Manuel mixed much more than the others, putting French words into their Spanish but not vice versa. This is common amongst the younger members of a large bilingual family. On the other hand, Trinidad never mixes – a fact the brothers cheerfully attribute to her spending more time helping her mother than they do! Trinidad is also the most positive about bilingualism, finding that it gives her a considerable advantage over girls who only speak Spanish.

The pattern in this family is, therefore:

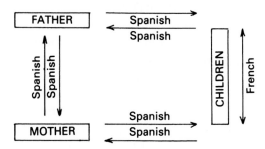

We would like to thank Florence Poncet and José Garcia for their help in carrying out Case Study 16.

Case Study 17: Single parent, two languages

Alice came to work in Brussels some ten years ago, at the suggestion of her sister, because it was easier to find work there than at home in the Philippines. Although she had a BSc in Elementary Education, she could not obtain a teaching post, partly because she was not a European citizen, partly because her French was too poor. Therefore, she has made a living as a baby-sitter, cleaner and domestic helper, working mostly for 'international' families, that is, people employed by the various European institutions or the multinational corporations based in Brussels. At the time of our conversation, for example, she had worked for a Danish family, a Dutch family and a French-English family. She usually speaks English with her employers and their children, having had a good grounding at school, but her first languages are Bicol, spoken in her home region (Naga), and the national language, Tagalog.

Not long after her arrival in Brussels, Alice met and had a relationship with a Filipino businessman and had a son by him, Alvin. However, the relationship did not work out and shortly after Alvin's birth his father left to work in the USA.

A doctor told Alice that she should only speak one language to her child, and she has tried to follow this advice, deciding on Tagalog as it was the most useful of her home languages: it is also widely spoken in the tightly knit Filipino community in Brussels, which has a variety of social activities centred around the Church. Alvin speaks Tagalog with a French accent and, although he makes mistakes, manages well when they return to the Philippines on holiday. He can also understand some Bicol, although Alice herself never speaks that language to him. Alvin started going to a crèche at the age of three months and French is certainly his first language, but now that he is nearly nine years old he says he enjoys speaking other languages and easily joined in the conversation in English. When he met his father for the first time last year in the USA, they spoke mainly in French with only a little English, although a year later it was difficult to establish clearly the reasons for this choice of language.

Alice has finally managed to obtain an official residence permit, and one of the families she works for has arranged French lessons for her, so she feels very positive about the future. With the help of his father, Alice can provide Alvin with a good education.

This case study amounts to a modified version of the third type of family in section 4.1. It illustrates that in cases where a child is brought up by one parent only, establishing bilingualism is perfectly possible – although it may be more difficult to maintain in some ways – as long as there is consistency in the pattern of use between the home language and the language of the world outside.

Case Study 18: Bilingualism in a 'reconfigured' family

Marie, who is French, met Manuel in Cuba while she was on one of a number of professional visits to the island. After some three years of seeing one another occasionally, they married in Cuba one Christmas. As Marie had a steady job at home and Manuel – a computer specialist – was pessimistic about his prospects in Cuba, they decided to make their home in France, along with David, who is Manuel's son by a previous marriage.

The saga of their tussles with their respective national administrations is long and complex, but in the end they found themselves living together as a family. At this point, Marie and Manuel had already learnt a little of one another's languages, but David, now aged thirteen, spoke almost no French at all. All three knew some English: Marie to a high level, as she was a qualified teacher of the language; Manuel was reasonably competent as he had needed it for professional purposes, and David had studied English for two years at school.

It had been quite clear to them from the beginning that they would form a bilingual family. None of them considered this a problem, and they frequently discussed how they would arrange it. Marie admits that she herself is something of a 'militant' in this respect, as she believes it is essential that both members of a couple should know the other's language well, and at the same time she was worried that if she and Manuel only spoke French to one another and Spanish to David, it would somehow 'isolate' him within the family unit. So they looked for various ways in which all three could learn and use both languages. Although they have been through various alternatives, the basic system that has emerged is the following: Marie speaks French to Manuel, he speaks Spanish to her, but when the three of them are together – at mealtimes, for instance – they speak Spanish.

Manuel always speaks with David in Spanish, and although occasionally David might reply in French – when the subject is school, for example – Manuel tries to get his son to repeat his message in Spanish. Marie now speaks to David mostly in French but, especially during the early stages when he was still learning French, he used to reply in Spanish, so they were on an even footing. Marie also encouraged him to use Spanish when he got stuck as the last thing they wanted was for him to feel that he couldn't communicate with them, above all if there was a problem.

It has to be emphasised that this arrangement is not a rigidly fixed one. Sometimes it is simply the person who initiates an exchange who decides what language will be used, and the others follow. Sometimes it is a matter of topic: if they are discussing a subject related to Cuba or 'something intimate' Marie and Manuel will speak Spanish to one another. And when Manuel was waiting to start a course of study at the local polytechnic, they agreed to speak mostly French so that he would advance more quickly. Once the course started, though, and he was surrounded by French all the time, they started using more Spanish again.

At the time of writing – fifteen months after his arrival in France – David speaks good French and he is improving all the time, although Marie has noticed that he sometimes misjudges the level of formality of a word or expression. For example, he may use the colloquial expressions picked up in the local volley-ball club as if they were technical terms. He has never complained about having to learn French; in fact he enjoys it when people praise the progress he has made. But at the same time he is ready to proclaim his Cuban identity, whether on T-shirts or in discussions at school. He keeps up his Spanish with visits to the cinema and by watching Spanish television, and he writes to his mother every week. In fact, the only real problem so far has been explaining to the school authorities that he did not want to follow Spanish classes; he wanted to do German. Marie and Manuel fully supported him in this, as they could see he would have been bored stiff doing simple grammar exercises in a language he already speaks fluently and that, apart from wasting his time, he was likely to become disruptive. None the less, they had a hard time persuading the teachers, who based their recommendation on the fact that he would get high marks. But for David this was irrelevant; he wanted to learn German because he had friends in Germany and because it was a subject he would start at the same time as all the other pupils, on a level playing field.

It is not clear that the way in which the members of this family use their languages has stopped evolving, but they have certainly developed the linguistic skills and the confidence necessary to make a success of their bilingualism, in the sense that they are very much in control of the situation.

III
An alphabetical reference guide

Accent

Up to the time when both languages are completely separated, some bilingual children go through periods during which they speak one of their languages with a foreign accent. This usually happens when one of the languages develops more quickly than the other because of the circumstances, for example, the child hears much more German than English and so speaks English with a German accent. This should not be any cause for concern: provided your child continues to receive sufficient practice in both languages, she will acquire the ability to speak both without an accent. Mockery or humour at the expense of the child's accent, even when meant affectionately, should be avoided at all costs as it might make the child anxious and self-conscious.

Children who undergo successive bilingualism (see p. 69) before the age of twelve to fourteen usually acquire perfect accents in the second language to be learnt, provided that the bilingual environment is maintained. With very few exceptions, adults are unable to acquire perfect accents, even when their ability to speak the language is native-like in every other aspect.

Parents should beware of expecting 'higher' standards of pronunciation from their children than they expect of themselves. Above all, avoid puristic (and unrealistic) nit-picking of the 'Did I hear you say often with a "t"?' type or pouncing on intrusive 'r's.

Age

Whether there is an ideal or optimal age to become bilingual is a question which has been debated extensively, and with mixed results. People can become bilingual at any age, but the way they go about it will be different, the areas of difficulty will be different and the eventual outcome is also likely to exhibit different characteristics (see *Accent*). Thus a decision about the optimal age is more likely to reflect an investigator's preference as to what constitutes an ideal bilingual, than offer useful guidance.

In bilingual families, the question of age usually does not occur. Two or more languages are a constitutive part of family communication and the children cannot help undergoing bilingual acquisition. Parents who try to control the age at which a child 'starts' acquiring the second language (on the assumption that it may be confusing or dangerous to have two languages from the start) often fail to obtain the desired result, and for reasons that are not surprising. If the mother stops speaking her language when addressing her child for two years, it will be very difficult for her to switch back to that language after such a long period and the child is very unlikely to see the point. If it is a question of *preventing* the child from seeing his grandparents or little neighbours who happen to speak the 'wrong' language, one wonders whether it is not the best recipe to make the child build up resentment *against* one or other of his languages.

In cases of successive bilingualism, where, for instance, a family goes abroad for an extended period with children of different ages, the difficulty can be that different educational systems have different expectations of children of the same age, so changing from one system to another may throw up problems. However, these are due to institutional requirements, rather than (st)age of acquisition in some objective or ideal sense. From this point of view, it often seems that the younger the better. Children who 'go abroad' early are fully assimilated in to the educational system of the foreign country. But children who move relatively late may well continue to prepare for their 'home country' examinations, which will often mean taking correspondence courses. On the other hand, adolescents are much faster learners than younger children and, given the motivation, become proficient in their second language much more quickly.

Differences in educational systems may or may not work to your advantage. In England, children start learning to read about a year earlier than in France, so that an English child arriving at the *cours préparatoire* (the first year of primary school in France) will be ahead on that front, which may be a considerable advantage if he has a lot to catch up on in French otherwise. Moving from France to England is likely to be much more difficult at about the same age. Note, however, that what really counts is age *in relation to* the social environment of the child and in particular in relation to the school environment. Starting school represents a major change in a child's life, who has to adapt to a new network of relationships and to extend his knowledge of the world beyond that of the family. It is not surprising that such a change, associated with a sudden change of language, should prove traumatic.

It is impossible to give hard and fast rules to parents in this situation, because of the multiplicity of possible cases. However, if children have to go to school in a foreign country, it seems preferable to put them in a class with roughly their own age group, even if this involves a lot of difficulty for a time. A child who feels he has been put with 'little ones' will not want to talk to them and will tend to hide his real linguistic problems behind disdain and aloofness while being thoroughly isolated and unhappy.

Lastly, it is essential to prepare children for the change and this can best be done as a family activity. It is not always possible to visit the country beforehand, but the more you familiarise yourself with the habits of the foreign community beforehand as well as with the language, the better. A positive attitude towards the foreign community can often be fostered by making friends with native speakers of the language.

Whatever their age, children who are suddenly transplanted to a new school environment and who hardly speak the language on arrival will need a period of adaptation of something like six to twelve months, that is, probably about the same length of time as their parents.

This period of adaptation-cum-acquisition is likely to be trying, punctuated by a number of crises such as discouragement, silence, despondency, frustration, homesickness and so on. However, these are likely to be compensated for by the children's realisation that they progress faster than their parents and that they do not retain the same accent.

Aptitude

Many parents raise the question about aptitude when they can compare their first child's development with the second's (or with another bilingual child of the same age). Differences can be striking, for instance, if the older child has apparently never found it difficult to separate both languages and the second produces a lot of mixed utterances. Could it be, then, that one is more *gifted* than the other towards becoming bilingual?

On the whole, research in this area has been inconclusive. Psychologists find it impossible to pinpoint what constitutes a 'gift for languages'; it can only be identified as a cluster of components that people can be shown to exhibit in varying degrees. Central characteristics seem to be the ability to discriminate the speech sounds of languages, the ability to relate speech sounds and their symbolic representation, grammatical sensitivity or the ability to interpret grammatical relationships from linguistic data intuitively, and capacity to memorise verbal material.

However, the view that the capacity to acquire language is universal does not invalidate the concept of language aptitude. People, after all, do differ widely in their achievement in their *first* language. In the same way, when it comes to a second language, it is likely that general cognitive skills and more specific abilities both play a part. But such notions of aptitude totally ignore the communicative and social features of language learning which are central to bilingual development.

Recent research on bilingual children strongly supports the view that, with a minimum of parental support, they have a significant advantage over monolingual children in those very areas of cognition involved in language learning, in that they are able to dissociate words from what they represent at a much earlier age.

However, this certainly does not mean that bilingual children are necessarily more 'gifted' than monolinguals for languages. Rather it seems the likely outcome of the nature of the language learning task they have to undertake in comparison with monolinguals. In fact, it is only a temporary 'advantage' and it does not predict eventual achievement at all.

Parents are advised to stop and think about the *actual* linguistic and interactional environment of a child before looking for hasty explanations about their ability to become bilingual. Relevant questions are: How much direct interaction in both languages does the child actually get? How often does the child go to the country of her second language? How many friends of her age has she in both languages? What are the child's other characteristics? Is she a good non-verbal communicator, for instance – a lot of children are very good at by-passing speaking altogether for a very long time, simply because they do not need it.

Secondly, parents should remember that independently of bilingualism, there are major differences in the rate of linguistic development from one child to another. In no case should parents indulge in the creation of a family myth that their child is not gifted for languages, as it could break her confidence when she is most likely to need reassurance and supportive attention.

Baby talk

'Baby talk' – the use of words such as 'potty', 'horsie' and 'sweetie' – is strictly a matter of personal preference, and has no influence on children's language acquisition.

On the other hand, the *way* you talk to babies is crucial. The fact that in all societies, mothers, fathers and caretakers instinctively change their speech to address their babies a long time before they can be reasonably expected to respond verbally, indicates that these modifications play a role in the development of the child as an interlocutor and partner. Typical modifications such as higher-pitched voice and exaggerated intonation, as well as high frequency of questions, all seem to have the function of helping the child acquire the 'give and take' of conversational skills. These are usually established by the time they are two years old and it is upon such skills that the process of language acquisition is dependent. It is to be noted that mothers – or women for that matter – do not have a special gift for this kind of talk. Any person trying to interact with a baby, including older children, achieves it by modifying their speech in the same way, naturally and subconsciously.

In a bilingual family, the sharing of a baby's time between both parents or between parents and a caretaker is probably the best way of ensuring the child's acquisition of the two languages.

Biliteracy

That a bilingual child should also become biliterate is important for a number of reasons:

The 'cultural heritage' aspect   Being able to read her 'other' language will give your child the opportunity of fully participating in her second cultural world. Biculturalism often finds its roots in the deep affection children develop for the characters who people their first books. Moreover, in spite of the growing tendency to 'internationalise' children's books, many tales and stories translate very badly.

The linguistic aspect   Reading will also give your child access to styles and varieties of language she would not meet otherwise. Particularly in cases where the family is a linguistic island within a foreign community, it is the best way of ensuring that the child's exposure to the language is not constrained by the linguistic habits of the family and its necessarily limited communicative routines.

The cognitive aspect   The written language gives children a tool to represent and manipulate their experience. Bilingual children, whose experience of the world is necessarily complex, need such tools perhaps even more than monolinguals. Reading in both languages makes a significant contribution to their developing higher levels of cognitive functioning.

Maintenance   Any bilingual child will have to engage in time-sharing between her two communities and / or languages. Given this predictable fact, reading both languages is probably the most precious tool you can give your child as it will help her maintain actively one language during periods when the other language is otherwise predominant. Lastly, from the moment a child can read, she can read what she wishes to read. This does not mean, of course, that parents should not have any control over their children's choice of books, but it does mean that the child may spend hours reading stories on topics you may not be interested in! The day you discover your seven-year-old knows all about the reproductive cycle of some insect you have never heard of, and tells you all about it in her weaker language, you may relax and sit back. The child's own curiosity and interests have become motivating enough for her to steer her own language development.

Helping a child become biliterate is very much like helping a child become literate with a few complications. Read to your child every day and if both languages alternate in the family, try to find a regular pattern (such as, Daddy's day followed by Mummy's day). It is also helpful to keep books on separate shelves, according to which language they are written in. Let the child follow the text while you read, particularly at the time when she starts learning to read the other language at school. Soon remarks will be made about the significant differences between the two languages. Philip (five years old) learning to read English at school says to his mother, reading a French story: *Tiens, tu ne dis pas le 't' à la fin des mots!* ('Funny that you don't say the "t" at the end of the words!').

Children's books and magazines are expensive. If you come across other bilingual families in your area, it can be useful to organise a little library in order to spread the cost, particularly when children reach the age when they enjoy magazines and start reading a lot. In the earlier stages, however, it is a good investment to build up a child's mini-library of favourites.

Code-switching

Of all the phenomena associated with bilingual acquisition, code-switching is the one that seems to be the most striking for outsiders. Far from being a problem, code-switching comes naturally to a child brought up by people addressing him in two different languages, whether it is in a one-parent / one-language type of family or in a home-language / outside-language environment. For example, a mother, who is French, arrives at the English childminder's house. Emma, who is three years and six months old, is playing in the living room. Emma says: '*Bonjour maman*'. She then turns to her childminder: 'Bye, I'm going now. See you'. In other words, the way a child switches codes reflects the way his two languages serve his communicative ends, and, from very early on, situations and people will be associated by the child with the use of one or the other of his languages.

What is interesting is bilingual children's early realisation that they can use code-switching itself as a means of communication in the bilingual environment. That they are aware of it is exemplified in the following exchange taking place in Emma's family, who live in England and use French as the family language. Emma insists on cycling in the kitchen around the table and has just cycled over her (English) father's toes.

> FATHER: *Emma, arrête de faire du vélo dans la cuisine* ('Emma, stop cycling in the kitchen').
>
> EMMA: *Non* ('No').
>
> FATHER: Stop cycling in the kitchen, I said.
>
> EMMA (climbs down from her bicycle, runs to her mother's arms and exclaims): Daddy talk English! (*sic*).

As they develop conversational skills, bilingual children also develop the ability to use this extra resource in more and more subtle ways, for pleading purposes, for marking intimacy or distance with interlocutors or to indicate they belong to or dissociate themselves from a group (see p. 63).

Once again, the child is likely to model his particular use of code-switching on that of the surrounding community and here a word of caution is needed regarding very small children. While code-switching – and particularly code-switching within utterances – requires highly developed skills and a deep knowledge of both languages, it also requires that both languages be grammatically made 'equivalent'. That is, if one wants to switch freely at any point between English and French, the equivalent structures 'I have given a toy to Paul' and *J'ai donné un jouet à Paul* will be chosen but not 'I have given Paul a toy'. It means that in the long run, if you indulge in a lot of code-switching, you tend to counteract the process of separation of the two languages at the grammatical level since you will necessarily favour those structures where both languages converge.

So, if you are a code-switching family, you must be aware of the fact that you are playing a subtle double game. You make your child's task easier by making obvious to him what both languages have in common, but you make it harder by minimising the importance of elements which are specific to each of the languages. Note that there is no reason why this type of linguistic input should be detrimental to the child's linguistic development if he has enough social contact with monolinguals of both his languages.

Colours

Different languages 'segment' the visible spectrum differently, for example:

Language A	1		2	3	4		5		6	
Language B	1	2		3	4	5		6		7

There can be a considerable lack of correspondence between the two sets of colour terms. When we are asked what colour a particular object is, we sort it into the nearest pigeon-hole, but objects which we sort into pigeon-hole 2 in language B might go into pigeon-hole 1 in language A.

Within Europe, colour-term differences are rarely as marked or as complicated as the example in the diagram. None the less, parents should not be too surprised if a colour *they* can clearly see is 'pale blue', say, is confidently described as 'green' or if 'orange' is labelled 'yellow'. All children can have trouble learning colours: the terms are arbitrary, there is no 'natural' (physical) point at which one colour is divided from another. Even two people with the same mother tongue can sometimes disagree as to what 'label' to give a particular colour. Bilingual children have an extra set of refinements to acquire; by and large, they seem to do so without any difficulty. However, although this field has in general been very thoroughly investigated (see, in particular, Berlin and Kay, 1969), we know of no published research that concentrates on the acquisition of separate sets by bilinguals.

Correcting

Although many people, especially teachers, have great difficulty believing it, there is no evidence that correcting helps people to learn.

We are using 'correcting' here in the limited sense of making a learner who has made a mistake repeat the right form or answer. So there is no need for the parents of bilingual children to feel that they should go in for incessant nit-picking. Indeed, there is every reason to believe that such behaviour is counter-productive: not only does it mean that communication in that language is being continually interrupted, but it can also actually put the child off speaking the language. If every time you open your mouth you find yourself being corrected, it is natural enough to decide to keep your mouth closed. As we have seen elsewhere in this book making mistakes is an essential part of the learning process.

The best way of helping your children learn a first or a second language is by providing them with the richest and most varied opportunities possible for hearing and using the language. By acting as a model, that is, by talking and interacting with your child, by playing and reading, singing, cooking and gardening together. The greater the quantity and quality of this 'input', the less you will need to correct. Quite unconsciously you will find yourself using the reformulations and providing the wide range of examples which really do help children learn.

Two final points: beware of puristic nonsense of the 'never end a sentence with a preposition' type; your child has enough to learn without imposing unnecessary and inaccurate drudgery of this kind. Secondly – but surely it goes without saying – no child should ever be punished (or even teased) for making linguistic mistakes.

Counting

Counting is a fundamental intellectual skill and one that parents therefore rightly regard as of considerable importance. Moreover, it is a skill that it is easy to identify and to check on and whose development can consequently be followed in detail.

The principles of counting are usually mastered between the ages of four and five, although here, too, there is wide individual variation.

As all experienced parents and teachers know, it is essential to distinguish between two different uses of the verb 'to count':

i) First, there is the ability to produce the words 'one', 'two', 'three', etc. in the right order, parrot-fashion.
ii) Secondly, there is the ability to describe groups of objects quantitatively on the basis of that order.

In other words, it is quite possible for a child to 'know her numbers' by heart, but not to be able to use them accurately or consistently in response to the question 'How many?'.

This is of interest from the point of view of the bilingual child's development, because whereas the child has to learn skill (i) for each language, she only has to learn skill (ii) once, since it is the same in each language and can therefore be transferred. (At least this is true where the same, decimal system is used in both languages, as is the case in Europe. It might not be true if two different systems were involved. However, we know of no research on this point.) This seems to be an example of a more general process: namely that intellectual skills ('notions', 'concepts') acquired in one language are also available to the child (if necessary) in the other language. In the case of simultaneous acquisition of the two languages, this may happen almost imperceptibly. Sometimes, though, the transfer can be quite dramatic: the child has learnt to count at home, say, and overnight (or so it seems to her teacher) starts counting at school in the other language. This is evidence that improving the home language can benefit the child's other language as well as her general cognitive development and is a justification, therefore, for maintaining the home language in most cases.

Some bilinguals have a preferred language for counting in. However, this is not an infallible guide as to which is their 'best' or 'real' or 'dominant' language, since it may just depend on a habit formed at school or the currency in question (you count francs in French, obviously!). Many other bilinguals (we would be tempted to say most, but have no firm proof) simply continue in the language they are already operating in.

Skills that are related to counting – superficially at least – are telling the time, the date and the days of the week. By and large, transfer also seems to operate here for the time and for dates, but we have come across several cases where it did not seem to apply to the days of the week. In the absence of statistical evidence on this topic, we can do no more than speculate that whereas 'one', 'two', 'three', etc. can be applied to any objects, 'Monday', 'Tuesday', 'Wednesday' can only be applied to the days of the week. If a French / English child lives in France, his free day in the middle of the week is *mercredi* not 'Wednesday'; not only does he experience this aspect of life in French, but Wednesday is not a free day in the English educational system.

Dictionaries

Dictionaries can be a great help in activities and games and picture dictionaries can be used before a child can read.

Parents should use different picture dictionaries for each of the languages spoken in the family. So-called 'bilingual' picture dictionaries have the enormous disadvantage of counteracting the child's differentiation of the two languages because they associate directly words belonging to two languages with only one picture. The fact that 'things' may have two labels is only one aspect of bilingual acquisition. First of all, these 'things' may be very different in the outside world (for example, French bread and English bread), a fact which explains the blandness or inadequacy of illustrations in such dictionaries, and secondly the meaning of the words in each of the languages may have completely different extensions (compare French *thé* and English 'tea').

As we have said before, bilingual children have an advantage over monolinguals in that they are given the chance of realising early on in life that linguistic signs are arbitrary – that 'a rose by any other name would smell as sweet'. But they also have to overcome the extra task of differentiating between the way these signs operate within each of their languages. One way of helping them do so is to use monolingual dictionaries from the very start, including the picture stage.

Doctors – and other 'authorities'

Some of our best friends are doctors, so we'd better be careful what we say. Or rather how we say it, since the basic facts are irrefutable: these are that bilingualism does not appear on the training syllabus of doctors, health visitors, nurses, social workers, or even psychologists and speech therapists. It makes as much sense to ask your doctor for advice about bilingualism as it would to ask him about your car.

Of course, some doctors do happen to know about bilingualism, just as some know about cars, but this only underlines the point that membership of a particular professional category does not guarantee this knowledge. In short, if you want to know about bilingualism and bilingual families, *ask bilinguals*, and do not be afraid to ask for a second opinion. For those of you who do not know any bilinguals (are you *sure?*) and for those who want a wide selection of types of bilingual family, this book is, we hope, a step in the right direction. But for putting the whole thing in its right perspective there is nothing like meeting other families who have been or are in similar situations to your own.

Readers may feel that the above is somewhat unfair to doctors, especially as there are examples in this book of doctors giving sensible advice, encouragement and support (see Case Study 3, for example). However, we know of far too many counter-examples for us to be able to leave the matter there. Apart from the minority of doctors (etc.) who are actually prejudiced against bilingualism (and who are often not above justifying their prejudices with airy references to experts and publications that do not exist), put yourself in the situation of the family doctor faced with questions on a topic for which he has had no specialist training. What is he to do? He has to give advice (at least, that is what is expected of him) and he has to play it safe. His advice, therefore, is just that: to play it safe, which for him will almost certainly mean telling parents that they should stick to one language.

What, then, are the qualifications necessary if one is to give advice about bringing up a family bilingually? We would suggest the following as a minimum:

i)   commonsense
ii) personal experience
iii) knowledge of bilingual families in general
iv) knowledge of this family in particular.

We would say that qualification (iv) implies that, when it comes to the crunch, the only people who can really take the decision to raise a bilingual family are the parents themselves. It is most unlikely that any outside expert or specialist could ever have the detailed knowledge about the family backgrounds and relationships, interests, tastes and personalities, aims and activities and plans for the future that such a decision involves. Not even linguists specialised in bilingualism can help you here, since so many of these factors are simply not linguistic: all they can do is give you a guided tour round town – qualification (iii). They can't decide for you which neighbourhood will suit you best. That decision is yours, but after all so are the children (and the effort!) involved.

Dreams

This is not a handbook on psychoanalysis, so we will only touch on one or two very limited aspects of this subject here. Firstly, we would like to scotch the widespread myth that 'the language you dream in is your real language'. This may seem harmless enough, but it is also inaccurate and tends to propagate further misunderstandings about the nature of bilingualism.

The fact is that if you ask bilinguals which language they dream in they will very rarely give you a clear-cut reply. The majority of them will say (again!): 'Well, it depends . . .' and if asked just what it depends on, they will give 'obvious' answers such as 'Who is speaking, or who I'm speaking to, or what I'm speaking about'. Perhaps less obvious, for the inquisitive monolingual anyway, is the reply: 'Well, it depends on *where* I'm dreaming: in Spain, I dream in Spanish, but in Germany, I dream in German'.

It is notoriously difficult to assess the value of what people say about their dreams and with young children the problem is only exacerbated. But even if we take the evidence at face value, it is so contradictory that one doubts if useful generalisations will ever be made in this field. For example, one small child in an English / French bilingual family living in France, but who never used a word of French at home, said she always dreamt in French, and that included speaking to her brothers and sister in her dreams. On the other hand, there are far too many reports – by both adults and children – of people dreaming in a language which they have only just come into contact with for us to accept the 'dream language / real language' hypothesis. Of course, such dreaming may well be a matter of wish fulfilment – though, again, dreamers report that their level of performance varies wildly – but this is not a real objection since it only emphasises our point that the situation is considerably more complex than the hypothesis would seem to indicate. It seems reasonable to suppose that during the time a second or third language is being learnt, it will be in some sense 'nearer the surface' and emerge into dreams more easily even if the dreamer's mastery of the language is limited. One small boy, who had just arrived in France and started nursery school, woke his parents with a few mighty yells in the small hours of the morning. When they appeared by his bedside he asked: 'What's the French for "spoon"?' On being told it was *cuillère*, he smiled, put his head on his pillow and was fast asleep again before his parents could leave his bedroom.

We will not pursue this subject. There has been no research done, so all that can be said is a mixture of anecdote and speculation. However, by the same token, we can state firmly that there is no evidence to support the old legend about bilingual children having more nightmares than others. For what it is worth, our impression (for it can be no more than that) is that bilingual children have no more and no fewer nightmares than monolingual children. Moreover, as we have seen, in many cases bilingualism is only one relatively minor aspect of the total disruption of the child's life in a new country, a new school, new friends: it is only to be expected that a child in such a situation should be upset, especially during the early transition stage. But to blame this on the language alone seems illogical, especially in view of the ease with which so many children learn a second language and of the fact that it is precisely the language which will help the child resolve so many of the problems (such as making new friends) with which she is faced.

Gesture – and non-verbal communication in general

A number of publications on 'body language' have appeared over the last ten to fifteen years, which have made the public in general more aware that communication is not just a matter of words. We communicate with our whole body, some of the most important factors being gesture, posture, facial expression, eye-contact and distance between speakers. Moreover, research has shown that, far from being 'instinctive' or 'universal', all these categories of non-verbal behaviour have to be learnt and are, in consequence, subject to variation from culture to culture.

The possibility exists, therefore, that just as an individual might speak two languages, he might also have two separate sets of non-verbal behaviour. This hypothesis has indeed been confirmed by numerous observers: probably the best-known example is that of La Guardia, Italian-American mayor of New York in the 1940s (see Efron, 1972). This example is famous partly because it was documented by a specialist, partly because the individual in question was a public figure. When he spoke Italian, he behaved like one, using far more hand- and arm-gestures, including a number which are never used by English speakers: the whole tempo and tonus of his movements changed.

It is not difficult to find bilingual children who exhibit two clearly different sets of non-verbal behaviour. Indeed, it can be quite surprising for unwary grandparents to *see* their English grandchild become French every time she speaks that language: her gestures are more frequent, rapid, precise and constrained, the pitch of her voice is higher and her physical behaviour generally conforms to French rather than English patterns.

On the other hand, having a different set of behaviours for each language is by no means invariably the case. Very many bilinguals indeed seem to have just one, generalised type of non-verbal communication. The problem is that we have little idea as to what the determining factors are in these matters. Even children in the same family may develop very differently in this respect.

Most bilinguals seem to have little trouble keeping the gestures known as 'emblems' apart. These are those gestures that are highly conventional, have a fairly precise meaning, and can easily be paraphrased or repeated. Examples in English which come to mind are 'thumbs up', 'the V-sign' and tapping your temple with your index finger to indicate that you think someone is 'mad'. These are clear-cut, conscious behaviours that are fairly easily controlled. But there are other aspects of our non-verbal behaviour – the way we talk or sit, for example, or signal an emotion – over which we have far less control and where, consequently, the bilingual is likely to 'give himself away'. To the extent that this means simply revealing something about his social identity, there is usually no harm done; giving yourself away is, as we have said, an act of communicative generosity. The problems begin where cultural differences in non-verbal behaviour result in misunderstandings, where the bilingual broadcasts the wrong message with his body.

However, we must keep a sense of proportion here; such misunderstandings are even more likely to occur between monolingual speakers of two different languages, and there can be no question about who is best-equipped to sort them out. Moreover people (especially young people) do learn, albeit unconsciously, to adapt their non-verbal communication much more rapidly than is generally realised. In an informal experiment run by one of the authors a few years ago, a small group of English-speaking students was observed for a period after their arrival in France. Within six or seven weeks all of them were making use of French non-verbal signals in communication, even when they spoke English.

Finally, it should be noted that none of the bilinguals we interviewed thought this was a problem: those who did spontaneously mention non-verbal communication did so because they thought the subject was fascinating or amusing. Of course, we had restricted ourselves to European / Western society: had we included more cases from Japan, say, or the Arab world, we might well have had very different reactions.

Internet

The Internet can be a great help to parents of bilingual families in several ways. The main one is to multiply occasions for communicating in writing with people but more especially for maintaining contact by e-mail with members of the family who speak the 'weaker' language. The motivation to communicate with grandparents and cousins can be very important at the moment when children start reading. It is a motivating medium because it is interactive and the urge to reply to messages is very strong. The short size of the messages exchanged encourages the beginners because it gives the impression that the task is of manageable size and, moreover, the informal tone somehow reduces the fear of 'making mistakes'. One of the drawbacks is that it is still often difficult to send and receive messages with the accents required by particular languages such as French, but it is a relatively small problem compared with the advantages.

The second way in which the Internet can be useful to bilingual families is that it can be a source of up-to-date information about language learning resources especially designed for young learners. Thirdly, it is a means of obtaining advice from professional associations more or less instantly and of joining associations of parents with whom one shares the bilingual family experience. Of course, parents need to be advised that as soon as access to the net is possible, the children develop their own networks and start developing imaginative ways of making use of it for all sorts of purposes – only some of which are related to their bilingual development. The reason why we think the Internet is so helpful is undoubtedly the resource it offers for communicating. Parents should never forget that language develops in the context of friendly and secure relations and these can be established and can be maintained easily with the net. It is primarily the social function of the net that is valuable although the extra resource it offers in terms of information should in no way be dismissed, particularly for parents who live abroad or in isolated areas. (See 'Internet sites', p. 180.)

Interpreting and translating

Some of the parents we interviewed whilst preparing this book already saw their children successfully interpreting at the United Nations. Proud grandparents and other relatives also seemed to imagine that being bilingual is in itself the guarantee of a glamorous job in later life. Now it may well be that the children in question will one day become interpreters and translators, but they will have to work very hard at it. The simple fact that one is bilingual is not in itself enough to make one capable of translation and interpretation, which are separate, specialised and different skills and which require an extremely high level of general knowledge.

In order to appreciate how specialised these skills are, consider just one example, simultaneous interpretation: it requires a considerable amount of training to listen to and understand one language whilst saying the translation of the preceding passage or remark in another, even for fluent bilinguals. To get an idea of just how difficult this is, try doing it in your first language only: for example, listen to the news on the radio and, as each item finishes, repeat the gist whilst at the same time listening to and memorising the following item. You will quickly realise that to do this in two languages is only to add further difficulty to what is *already* an extremely difficult task.

Interpreters and translators have to strive hard to achieve the levels of speed and accuracy required of them. For many people they are the only 'true' bilinguals, but this is like saying that only Formula 1 drivers really know how to drive: nobody can deny that they do it faster and more accurately than most people, but most people do, after all, manage perfectly well. The fact is that most bilinguals do not need the specialised skills and levels of performance of professional interpreters and translators.

Lastly, it is important to note that top professional translators and interpreters are in fact highly specialised, often dealing with only one restricted area such as biochemistry or marine law. People often mention with awe the fact that a top-flight congress interpreter will only work for about three hours a day: they attribute these 'cushy' hours to the incredible strain placed on the interpreters, which is certainly true. But what they do not realise is that an interpreter's 'free time' is devoted to an intensive study of the latest developments of the specialisation in question: to be able to interpret, you first have to be able to understand. Bilingualism, therefore, is not enough: you also have to be an expert on the topics being discussed and to have undergone specialised training.

Mixing

Parents are often concerned when their child produces mixed utterances. They fear it may be a sign that the child is confused. Very few case studies of bilingual children, however, report complete differentiation of both languages from the outset. On the contrary, most concentrate on the way the child shows evidence of gradually separating the two language systems. This process seems to occur at different stages and at a different rate for different levels of language: sound structure, vocabulary, grammar, meaning. For instance, although the separation of the two sound structures seems to start earlier than that of the grammatical systems, mastery of fine pronunciation differences such as the production of initial 'p', 't' and 'k' in French and English is not achieved until about the age of six.

Mixed utterances have to be seen as part of this process of gradual separation. The main trouble, in reality, is that they stand out and are often the subject of remarks by outsiders. If you do worry, a bit of arithmetic can help: calculate the proportion of mixed utterances produced by your child as compared to her utterances produced in each of the languages. In a typical bilingual family where each parent addresses their child in a different language, the chances are that a two-and-a-half-year-old child produces between 80 and 90 per cent of her utterances to Mummy in her language, between 80 and 90 per cent of her utterances to Daddy in his language, and the remaining 10 to 20 per cent are mixed. The size of the 'problem' is thus put in perspective.

As to the nature of the 'problem', close observation often permits us to discard the confusion argument. Most 'mixed utterances' are simply words inserted in a structure belonging to the other language. Often the word in question has just been heard in her other language or the child is talking about an experience she has lived 'through' the other language and for which she simply does not know the equivalent in her second language.

Mixed utterances are also likely to coincide with moments when a child is progressing linguistically and in particular when the child is analysing chunks she has produced 'correctly' before by simple imitation. For example, Emma (3 yrs, 6 mths, English / French) used to produce 'very much' in English and *beaucoup* in French. Within three days she produced 'very better' in English, *beaucoup mieux* and *très beaucoup* in French as well as 'very *mieux*' for good measure. This is not worrying but rather a sign that she is acquiring two complex sub-systems in both grammars. The best medicine is clearly to provide her with the correct forms until she gets them right.

The relevant question is, then, how do you help your child differentiate between her two languages? There are three common-sense ways of doing this. First, it is a good idea to keep both languages clearly separated within the family, not only by being consistent in addressing the child, but also when talking to one another. This is not always easy. Bilingual parents tend to produce a lot of mixed utterances themselves often for ease of reference, for example: 'I was going to the *Galerie Lafayette* this morning. I had just come out of the *Station Chaussée d'Antin* when I realised I had left my shopping list in *rue Voltaire*'. Secondly, if a child produces mixed utterances, do not reprimand her or engage in a tedious 'repeat after me' type of exercise. Provide her instead with what she could have said had she talked to you in the language you normally use together, for example:

EMMA: Maman, I want to go *dans la piscine* again.
MOTHER: *Ah! Tu veux retourner dans la piscine? Eh bien vas-y!*

Thirdly, try to multiply occasions when the child is in contact with people she likes but who truly understand only one of her languages. The child's desire to communicate with them will naturally make her discard those elements in her speech that apparently are not understood.

Once two languages are established, the problem is of a different nature. From that moment on, one can properly talk of dominance of one language over another. There are times when the predominance of one language, in terms of amount of use, leads to that language influencing production in the temporarily weaker language. This could be compared to the difficulties of monolinguals coming back to work or college with a local accent after a long holiday 'back home'. But here it is the long-lasting problem of maintenance with which bilingual individuals have to come to terms. Solutions are many, from listening to the radio to reading every day and / or keeping up a lot of correspondence, but it is a fact that languages are like musical instruments: without practice, temporary clumsiness can be expected when next they are taken up.

Names

Many parents like to choose names for their children that are familiar to and can be pronounced by both sides of the family. *Philippe Michel* in France (and in French) becomes 'Philip Michael' in England (and in English). This seems to us to be a reasonable but by no means essential measure. In any case, it is not one that is always possible, even in Europe where there is a pool of 'international' names like Paul, Frederic or Barbara.

It is important, of course, to avoid accidental connotations of an unfortunate kind, whether of sound or meaning, but who is better placed to do this than a bilingual couple, provided both sides have their say. One thinks, for example, of the English-speaking husband who wanted his 'French' daughter named *Marie-Rose*, until his wife explained to him that that is the name of the pungently vinegary patent medicine used universally in France for the treatment of lice.

As an insurance, of course, you can always give your child several first names, possibly reflecting his mixed background, leaving him and everyone else concerned a free choice. Who knows, the future may see an increase in 'hybrids' such as Graham Otto or Maryse Sheila.

The pronunciation of surnames can be a slight problem: what usually happens is that children adopt two different versions of their names, one for each language. Where this is possible it saves time and trouble spelling and explaining. 'Riley', for example, becomes *Rilé*. This sometimes bothers their parents, but never seems to trouble the children. Unfortunately, it is not possible to do this with the name of your place of birth: Emily Riley, for example, finds it 'a real nuisance' spelling out 'Jyväskylä, Finland' – 'and insisting on all the dots'. She is now the proud possessor of a document issued by the French Ministry of Education, assuring her that she was born in *Jyväskylä, Grande Bretagne*!

Finally, it is worth noting that some children actually like having a name that is out of the ordinary. Here, as elsewhere, the matter is not just a linguistic one, but depends on such factors as the individual child's personality.

Nationality

As we hope this book makes clear, your nationality has nothing to do, legally speaking, with the language you speak. It is quite possible to speak French without being French. In many cases, it is also possible to have two nationalities – German and English, for example – without speaking both languages perfectly. (All this seems terribly obvious, of course, to bilinguals.) Problems concerning your children's nationality should be addressed to consuls and ambassadors, not to linguists!

Other languages

We do not know if there is a maximum number of languages that a human being can learn. Stories of phenomenal achievements in this field abound, though hard evidence is not always so easy to come by. A well-attested present-day example, though, is George Schmidt, of the United Nations Translation Department in New York City who, according to the *Guinness Book of Records*, 'can reputedly speak fluently in 30 languages and has been prepared to embark on the translation of 36 others'. Sir Richard Burton, the nineteenth-century explorer, could speak over 25 languages (see Brodie, 1967) – a particularly impressive performance when one remembers that in many cases a slip would have cost him his life (although on his famous trip to Mecca 'he travelled as an Indian Pathan to allow for any peculiarities and defects in his speech'!).

What we do know is that even such exceptional individuals are far from exhausting the storage capacity of the human brain, according to recent work. More modest examples are easy to find: at a professional meeting of 160 European specialists held in Denmark in 1983, the *average* number of languages spoken by each of the participants was three or four (in fact the only monolinguals present were speakers of English or French). The parents of bilingual children do not need to worry about their offspring being over-loaded by learning a third, fourth or fifth language in or out of school.

It has often been noted that bilinguals have a positive, confident attitude towards the learning of other languages. This is not very surprising. Although bilinguals may vary in their interest for languages, the very fact that they have mastered two languages makes them feel that there is no reason why they should not succeed in learning a third or a fourth one. Learning languages makes you good – at learning languages. This conclusion will come as no surprise to anyone who has tried to master other skills such as playing tennis, the piano or chess.

Their bilingualism gives children an interest in and an insight into languages in general, which provides them with a head start when they tackle a new language. The bilingual child already knows subconsciously many of the things about language that present problems to the monolingual child. The most important of these is that other languages are different, and that it is no good asking 'why' all the time. A 'car' is a *voiture* is a *bil* and that is all there is to it. The same goes for the rules of grammar, idioms and sounds.

There are other reasons why a bilingual child starting a new language will do better than other children. Depending on the languages in question, he may find he has a large amount of vocabulary 'for free', for example. The children in our study who were old enough to have started languages at school nearly all reported that they were complimented on their accents; partly this is a question of attitude, partly it is a matter of having two repertoires to choose from.

However, before we raise any false hopes, let us emphasise that having a head start does not mean that bilingual children will not have to work thereafter just as hard as their classmates to learn a language at school. Indeed, in some cases, there is clear evidence that early success leads to over-confidence, resting on laurels and a consequent falling-off in performance.

It is important to understand, too, that the way in which a child learns a language at school has very little in common with the ways in which bilingual children learn their languages at home. This is not in itself a criticism of school methods; the two situations are so entirely different that the method cannot be the same. At home, the child has at least one full-time 'teacher' available for 'private lessons'. At school, there is one teacher for a few hours a week with 20–30 pupils. Bilingual children starting a language at school are usually astonished by the way the language is taught, *whatever the method.*

Emily (trilingual French / English / Swedish) has come back from school. She has just started German and is very excited about it.

> EMILY: Daddy! Daddy! Do you know how they teach languages at school?
> FATHER: Er – no love. Why? What's it . . .
> EMILY: It's funny. It's ever so funny. The teacher says a phrase and then she goes round the whole class and all of you have to say the same phrase five times!
> FATHER: Good heavens! And what was the phrase?
> EMILY: I've forgotten.

Reactivation of 'dormant' languages

Parents are sometimes concerned when one of their children's languages appears to have gone 'dormant'. This tends to happen when circumstances lead to a change in the pattern of use of both languages. Such parents should be reassured; the language is there and can be reactivated. That 'recovery' of language structure and of skilful discourse performance in the 'dormant' language can be remarkably speedy has been documented by Ulrike-Kellett and Alarcon-Neve (2001). They give the example of a six-year-old Spanish / English bilingual living in England whose Spanish had become effectively passive after she had started school in England to the extent that she switched to English to talk to her sibling. She achieved recovery of her first language (Spanish) in a month during a visit to Columbia, progressing from two- and three-word utterances to full conversations in Spanish making use of complex sentences. In the case of an eight-year-old Spanish / German bilingual who had lived in Austria between the ages of two and five, full narrative skills in German were observable after daily story-telling in both languages for two months and two weeks' immersion in a German / Spanish environment.

Reading

Reading in two languages does not seem to be a major problem. If a child learns to read in one language at school, she will normally transfer her developing reading skills to the second language without great difficulty, particularly if the writing system is the same (see the entry *Script / writing system* below for other cases). A father who had been very careful not to teach his seven-year-old son to read English, so as to avoid confusing him as he was learning to read in French at school, was amazed to find the request 'Can I try?' followed by an accurate, rhythmic reading of the next paragraph of a book in English. The boy knew how to speak English, he had learnt how to read, so he read English.

Recent research suggests that the social context within which the bilingual child first experiences the activity of reading may be crucial. Herman (1996) has shown that bilingual children's story-telling ability in their second language depended on their experience of stories in that language at home. Bialystock (2001) comments: 'The importance of reading stories to children turns out to have implications beyond the general effects of introducing literacy – it develops as well a language-specific competence in the language of those stories'.

Three broad stages are proposed by Bialystock to describe the development of reading in bilingual children and the different levels of skills each of them require: At the 'pre-literacy stage' there is strong evidence that bilingual children have a significant advantage over monolingual children because their experience offers them more opportunities to understand the fact that the written language is a symbolic representation of the spoken language. The second stage is that of 'early reading'. It is at this stage that the rules relating the form of the written to the spoken forms of the language are acquired and also the stage when language-specific aspects are most likely to play a role. It is also the period when the child needs most encouragement and support. The third stage is that of 'fluent reading' when the meaning of what is read takes priority. As in all domains of bilingual performance, it is crucial to remember that there are important individual differences between children and also that, not surprisingly, performance is related to familiarity with the language. There is evidence that bilinguals tend to read more slowly in their 'second language', but this can change with circumstances and in any case, as Bialystock writes, 'not too bad a price for being able to read!'.

Refusing to speak the language

Everyone seems to have come across cases where a bilingual child refuses to speak one of the two languages. However, in the cases we studied, there were no unequivocal examples of this situation. Keep in mind, though, that we are not talking about cases where there is social tension between the two communities: for example Claire, an English / French / German trilingual, recalls in the early 1940s 'refusing to speak English' with her English mother, who persisted in communicating with her daughter in that language – bang in the middle of occupied Paris! To attribute this refusal to deep-seated psychological problems would really be rather perverse.

None the less, we feel we have to deal with this topic here, if only because it is so emotive. It is just like children refusing to eat their food and arouses the same mixture of anger and a sense of rejection in the parents. Before simply abandoning the language in question, though, you would do well to consider the following points:

i) Is it simply a temporary whim? After all, monolingual children also sulk, refuse to answer, throw tantrums and so on. If it is, you still have a problem on your hands *but* it is short term and not due to a linguistic difficulty.

ii) Is it *you* who is breaking the rules in some way, such as (in families who have a home-language / outside-language pattern) using the language outside the home?

iii) Are non-speakers of the language present? Children can be very sensitive about this, although for different reasons. They may just suddenly feel shy, not wanting to appear different in front of friends. Or, and this is common, it may be an expression of natural politeness and warmth, where they feel upset about leaving someone out of the conversation. In such cases, some kind of compromise is usually possible, such as speaking the visitor's language except for any remarks directed by the parents to the child individually. However, many families we spoke to completely adopted the visitor's language for the duration of the visit.

iv) Most of the advice given in this book is rather tentative, but one point we feel can be stated categorically, since it was made spontaneously and repeatedly *by the children themselves*: children should never be asked to 'show off', to 'say something in (French, Swedish, Japanese)' simply for the benefit of a visitor, inspector or friend, and if the request is initiated by the visitors, they should be firmly protected from this well-meaning curiosity. Several children in our study chose this as the *only* disadvantage they could think of in being bilingual. Younger children find 'saying something' excruciatingly embarrassing and totally unnatural. Older children adopt different tactics, such as having a set expression ready (sometimes unprintable), or 'complying' in the minimal way possible:

– *C'est vrai que tu parles l'anglais? Dis quelque chose en anglais, vas . . .* ('Is it true that you speak English? Go on, say something in English . . .')

– No (in English).

v) Is the child a receptive bilingual only? That is, is his comprehension far better than his expression? (See section 3.1.) Such cases are extremely common and should not be written off as a wilful refusal to speak, which is most unfair to the child, who is not responsible for his situation. Instead parents should consider their options. One possible option is to simply accept this state of affairs, knowing that if the child ever does really want or need actually to speak the language the transition can be made easily and rapidly. Another option is to take a closer look at the child's linguistic situation to see in what ways expression can be encouraged and maintained.

vi) Is the child going through a phase of refusing to compete with an elder sibling or of asserting his own identity? If so, the problem will be resolved, but only when those things change, which may take very different lengths of time.

In general, then, it is important to distinguish between 'refusing to speak' on a particular occasion or occasions – cases (i)–(iv) – and longer-term 'refusals' – (v) and (vi). Where the child really seems to have acquired a thorough dislike of the language, there seems little point in insisting, though such cases seem, on examination, to be rare. Not only will a child whose attitude to a language is negative fail to learn it, but making the child's life a misery is not a reasonable price for bilingualism. However, there is no reason why the parents should change *their* linguistic pattern either. In many cases, this will mean accepting replies in a language other than the one they address the child in; in other words, settling for receptive bilingualism – a practical compromise that has the advantage of keeping options open.

School

This book is written for bilingual families where – one way or another – the pattern of use and consequently the children's language acquisition involves two languages. It is worth repeating here that this book is not about bilingual education principles and policies. In other words, the political and social issues relating to the kind of programmes that exist in a number of countries to address the educational needs of linguistic minorities fall outside the scope of this handbook. You can find excellent treatments and critical discussions of these issues, for example, Romaine (1995, Chapter 6), Baker (2001) or Jorgensen and Holden (1997). Obviously, in some cases, bilingual families come to live in or to visit bilingual areas like Alsace, or countries like Canada or Wales, where they need to take into account the way societal bilingualism has been addressed in the school system. This reinforces the point: the number of factors that determine parents' decisions regarding schooling in any given context and for one particular child is so large that we feel it is impossible to give definite guidelines. Instead, we offer below a few guiding principles which may be of use to parents when they are considering their options. In general terms, they are based on the idea that the parents are not just trying to support the development of both languages in their children but that they are aware that their parental role is crucial in helping their children forge a secure and harmonious bilingual and bicultural identity. From this vantage point, the question becomes: What can we do to work with the school to support our children's development and are there 'critical' moments when we should be particularly attentive? The following is organised in three stages corresponding broadly to the three stages identified by Bialystock (2001) for the development of biliteracy (see *Reading*).

At the playgroup stage, what really counts is that children have many occasions to use both languages in as wide a range of situations as possible. If your child is acquiring both languages simultaneously and starts going to a playgroup where she uses only one of them, it is a good idea to inform the teacher about the bilingual experience of the child so that a climate of co-operation is established. This is also a moment when parents might see the language of the playgroup 'jump ahead of the other language' and decide to give priority to activities in the other language at home to avoid too much of a gap between the development of skills and fluency in both languages. The situation may be more difficult to manage in cases of consecutive (or successive) bilingualism. Such cases frequently occur when families move abroad for a few years. Not surprisingly, the experience of being plunged into a group of people who do not speak their language can be puzzling for children – although very young children seem to cope much more easily than their parents! These are moments when the children need reassurance and when it may be more important than ever to maintain the home language routines such as story-telling, because they provide emotionally reassuring occasions where use of the home language acts both as a marker of a shared history and as a symbol of the permanence of the relationship. It is also preferable not to start speaking the new language to your child when at home. The emotional importance of associating parental relations with one particular language should not be underestimated and one can easily imagine how the stress at school coupled with a sudden switch at home may be construed by the child as a kind of denial, particularly at a moment of general upheaval for the whole family. Listen to the advice of this 38-year-old bilingual interviewed by Arnberg (1987: 148): 'My personal opinion is that parents should speak the language they know best to their children. Only in this way can they convey their innermost thoughts and feelings to their children'.

At primary school level, the same principles apply. In the first years, the main area of monitoring concerns the child's reading development (see *Reading* and *Biliteracy*). If the child refuses to read in the 'second' or 'home' language, it is best not to insist and turn it into a big thing but to maintain home reading routines unperturbed, selecting 'favourite' stories whenever possible. In many countries, your child may be able to take advantage of small reception classes organised for children who have just arrived and do not speak the language. In my experience, in Europe, these multilingual classes – usually taught by specialised staff – are very successful. While they bring together children who share the problem of having to learn the same new language, they typically encourage them to value their linguistic and cultural diversity and to use their home language within the family. In the context of schools and the schooling system, parents should be aware of potential difficulties in understanding the meanings of certain 'labels'. First, conversations with teachers or local parents can be very confusing. If you arrive in the UK, the words 'KS1', 'KS2' and 'KS3' (meaning Key Stage 1, 2, 3) will constantly occur in conversations to refer to the level of attainment specified by the government and for which children are tested at particular ages, while French teachers and parents happily refer to CE1(*Cours élémentaire première année*) or CM2 (*Cours moyen deuxième année*), which of course correspond respectively to the Scottish P3 and P4 (Primary 3rd and 4th Year) and P6 and P7 (Primary 6th and 7th year)! Similarly, although it is not always easy to achieve when arriving in a new country, it is worth checking precisely what certain phrases or labels such as 'Bilingual classes' or 'Bilingual programmes' actually mean locally. These have become popular in many European countries in the past ten years, and while certain schools do promote bilingualism effectively with subjects being taught via the medium of another language, other schools may in reality provide nothing more than a reinforced second-language programme which may be totally inadequate – and incredibly tedious and demotivating – for a child who is effectively a native speaker of that language. Lastly, it is important to check on possible inconsistencies in the system and their pedagogical medium-term consequences; do not hesitate to ask for detailed information on the transition to the secondary level for children who have had a bilingual programme at primary level.

At secondary school level, the general scheme of things becomes much more complicated because, apart from exceptional circumstances where there are appropriate bilingual programmes, your child will be expected to attend classes in modern languages and those may be totally unsuitable. If your child has been put in a language class where the others are beginners in one of his languages, the best thing to do is to discuss possible strategies with the school. It is often possible for the child to start a new language but this is a solution that does not resolve the problem of the further development of his second (home) language. In one such case, it was agreed with the school that the bilingual pupil would attend the modern language classes in his home language but would use the class time to read books. It was a boosting experience for the child whom the other pupils could see enjoyed reading in the language they were only just beginning to tackle, but also, crucially, an introduction to reading as an intellectual discipline associated with the acquisition of knowledge in a formal context (Snow et al., 1991). Choices at that level are determined by the parents' expectations concerning their whereabouts or circumstances in the foreseeable future, the examination systems in particular countries, the school's room for manoeuvre and the children's inclinations. Parents need to know that the language within which children experience adolescence and their teenage friendships is likely to remain their preferred language. If it becomes the language in which they study or work as well, it is predictable – and not very surprising – that they will become dominant in that language.

Script / Writing system

When bilingual children are introduced to reading and writing, their task is made more complicated if the two languages have different scripts, for example the Roman script and the Cyrillic script. This is particularly crucial in the very first stages where the child needs to grasp the symbolic nature of print and what it stands for. To estimate the size of the difficulty encountered by children who need to master the rules that relate print and spoken language, it is useful to make the difference between 'scripts' and 'writing systems' (Coulmas, 1989). Whereas the difficulty associated with decoding two different scripts is a question of notation, the difficulties associated with two different writing systems are of a different order because they refer to the particular aspect of linguistic structure that serves as a basis for representing the spoken language. Thus, in an alphabetic system, there is a systematic relation between the letters of the alphabet and the sounds of the language but in character systems the basis is a word. There is clear evidence that, initially, children learning to read in English and Hebrew (which have different scripts but share an alphabetic writing system) have an easier task than children learning to read English and Chinese (which have different writing systems). This is one of the reasons why it would be a mistake to assume that reading performance in both languages should be necessarily equivalent or that it can be predicted on the basis of oral fluency.

Bilingual children who learn to read two different systems or scripts seem to follow the same path to literacy as other bilingual children. When reading in their second language, they may transfer strategies acquired for reading their first, which native speakers of the second language would not normally use, although this can only be detected by sophisticated psychological experiments. As a parent, it is useful to be aware that your child may need a lot of support in both languages in the very early stages and to be ready to accept that she may simply decide to delay trying to read the second language – at least temporarily.

Spelling (see also *Writing*)

Generally speaking, the more a child reads, the more likely she is to reach a reasonable level in writing and spelling. Many parents regard accuracy of spelling in the second (non-school) language as being of only minor importance. Moreover, they feel that a child who is at school all day learning to read and write Language A really can't be expected to start all over again in Language B when she gets home. None the less, many bilingual children do *want* to learn to write their second language, just as monolinguals often start 'playing school' the minute they get home. In such cases, if the parents can find a way of making it fun, all well and good.

A blackboard in the kitchen and a list of games and activities, including some that the child can get on with without interrupting your own work, is a good idea. Alternatively, if there are problems of space, you can buy magnetic alphabets which do marvels on the side of the fridge. Scrabble,

Boggle, crosswords and Hangman all help to improve spelling and extend vocabulary. When playing Hangman, let your child use the dictionary to find really difficult words for when it's your turn to guess. You can also ask your child to write down all the words she can think of which contain / start / finish with a particular sound. For example, in French, there are the various ways of writing the nasal sound one hears in the second syllable of the word *maman: -en, -an, -ent, -ans, -ant, -aon.*

Another useful technique is to invent a story for the child which she has to write down. You can adapt it to her age and level and can make it stop at a moment of suspense when you see the child is getting tired. Below is an example from a seven-and-a-half-year-old English / French bilingual living in England. Philippe had just read *Le Petit Prince* by Saint Exupery and wrote his own version:

Le rêve de Philippe

C'est la nuit. Philippe dort dort dans sa chambre bleue. Il fait chaud dehors. La fenêtre est overte. Tout a coup, le rideau se gonfle. Est ce le vent? Non. C'est un petit garçon blond, qui saut par la fenêtre, comme chez lui. "Philippe? Philippe!" "Quoi?" "Tu as l'air gentille. Veux tu venir jouer chez moi? "Mais, qui est tu?" Est ce que tu veux venir? On va jouer ensemble." "Mais, je ne peux pas quitter la maison." "Pourquoi? Est ce que tu ne veux pas être mon ami?" "Si, mais qu'est ce que mes parents vont dire?" "Tes parents?" Silence. "Ca ne fait riens. Viens! "D'accord. Ou va t'on?" Chez moi. depèche toi le vole est long!" "Ah! Attends. j'ecris a maman

Philippe's dream

It is night time. Philippe is sleeping in his blue bedroom. It is warm outside. The window is open. Suddenly, the curtain swings into the room. Is it the wind? No. It is a fair-haired little boy who jumps from the window as if he were in his own home.

– Philippe! Philippe!
– What?
– You seem to be nice. Do you want to come and play with me?
– But who are you?
– Do you want to come? We'll play together.
– But I cannot leave the house!
– Why? Don't you want to be my friend?
– Yes, but what are my parents going to say?
– Your parents?

(Silence.)
– It doesn't matter. Come on!
– OK. Where are we going?
– To my place. Hurry up! The flight is long!
– Ah! Wait! I'm writing to Mummy.

The following day, Philippe was asked to find mistakes in his story and was able to correct most of them himself by reading the story aloud again.

This example is given because Philippe has had no formal training in French apart from a three months' spell at the *cours préparatoire* when he was six. It shows that the kind of activities described above coupled with a lot of reading can achieve good results as far as spelling is concerned.

Stuttering

The British Stammering Association (www.stammering.org) was able to confirm to us that to date, there is insufficient evidence to suggest a direct link between stuttering and bilingualism, despite the popular belief to the contrary. Nor do countries with a high proportion of bilinguals have significantly higher statistics on stutterers than monolingual countries. Perhaps it is useful here to remind parents that the proportion of stutterers is estimated to be only 1 per cent of the world population (Bloodstein, 1995).

However, there is possibly an indirect link between the two phenomena. It seems that many children go through a period of disfluency. If, during this period, the child is made self-conscious or anxious about his speech, this could add to the demands put on the planning and encoding process and might lead to stammering if a predisposition towards developing these problems exists. In social situations, a bilingual child may find it stressful to have to choose which language to use and if members of the family make remarks or laugh at him if he selects the 'wrong' language, or if he has some difficulty expressing himself in his weaker language in front of strangers. Again, if the predisposition is there, the added strain could lead to stammering.

It is obvious that bilingual children tend to attract more attention than monolingual children, in that they are often regarded as a bit of a phenomenon. Their speech is commented on by adults who would never dream of subjecting a monolingual child's speech to the same scrutiny. Whether the comments are favourable or not, this tends to exaggerate the importance of what is, for the child, perfectly natural and automatic behaviour. A source of profound embarrassment is the adult who insists on speaking to the child in, say, excruciatingly rusty school English when it would be far more natural and efficient for them both to speak French. On several occasions, we have witnessed adults dismissing some poor child's bilingualism as a myth 'because I spoke to him in English (etc.) and he didn't understand a word' without seeming to realise for a second that this was a criticism of their own English (and the inappropriacy of their language choice) rather than the child's. At such times, it really is up to parents to come to the rescue: 'You know, love, Mr X also speaks very good French'.

All parents should be aware of the following rule, which is valid for bilinguals and monolinguals alike: if your child shows any signs of disfluency, don't respond with impatience or irritation. You should even avoid correcting what he says, as this only serves to focus his attention on the way he talks rather than on what it is he is trying to convey. On the contrary, you should make a special effort to make talking as enjoyable as possible for the child, both by being a good listener and by introducing topics that interest him, so as to build up his self-confidence.

The following additional advice seems to be in order for the parents of bilingual children:

i) The less fuss made about your child being bilingual, the better.
ii) If your child shows any signs of disfluency:

If the disfluencies occur in only one language and your child's speech is characterised by frequent hesitations and repetitions, do not fret: the issue may simply be one of imbalance between his proficiency in his languages, so that he does not have the words in one of the languages to talk about what he experiences in the other language. This is a frequent phenomenon when the home language is different from that of the school. It may be the moment when you need to give a 'boost' to the weaker language. It may be sufficient to read stories that provide the child with the vocabulary he needs; for example, choose a story that takes place in a school.

Do not believe that the solution is to make the child stop speaking one of his languages, particularly the home language, as this is likely to be counterproductive: it will increase your child's anxiety and will instil in him the belief that something is definitely wrong with his speech. In cases where there are brothers and sisters who are perfectly fluent in both languages, such a strategy could be particularly disastrous.

If the disfluencies become a serious problem and in particular if you notice that they are accompanied by noticeable tension, eye blinks or body movements (see Watson and Kayser, 1994) your child may be an incipient stutterer. It is wise to consult a speech therapist as soon as possible since intervention is most effective the sooner it occurs after onset. Speech therapists are experienced in distinguishing between stuttering and other types of disfluencies and they are trained in ensuring that the child's attention will not be drawn to the speech problem. But if you do not have access to one who is bilingual in the same languages as the child, be aware that 'it is not known if or how well clinicians are able to make reliable or valid judgments about the presence of stuttering in languages or dialects other than their own' (Van Borzel et al., 2001).

Swearing

Four-year-old Katja (trilingual Swedish / English / French) is sitting on the living-room rug, playing with her toys and talking to herself. Suddenly she exclaims: '*Oj-oj-oj* – oh dear, oh dear – *merde!*' Where a Swedish-speaking or an English-speaking observer would find this quite harmless, or even charming, most French speakers would be slightly shocked to hear the word for 'shit' produced by a tot. Katja's problem is that she has come up against one of the four 'great untranslatables', that is, jokes, poetry, menus and swearing, where the interplay between culture and language is often unique.

To the obvious objection that there *is* a direct and adequate translation (*merde* = 'shit') we must ask you to put yourself in her position: she knows that she should not say 'shit' because her parents tell her off when she does so: so she has classified it amongst the 'rude words'. But she has learnt her French playing with children, and like children everywhere, they revel in breaking the taboos when out of adult earshot. So she has never been socially conditioned in the same way about *merde* as she has about 'shit'. Or, to put it more simply, one is a swear-word for her, the other is not – although both 'mean' the same thing. So she has classed *merde* along with the harmless exclamations *oj-oj-oj* and 'oh dear!'.

Parents should not be surprised if this is a problem that crops up early in their stay in a new country. Swear-words are easy to learn and children soon realise they are 'special'; moreover, they allow the new child to show that she is 'one of the crowd'. Although it may be difficult to do so at the time, parents should regard such early swearing as a first step towards integration. This does not mean, though, that they should encourage it or even condone it. The child should be informed as clearly and as simply as possible (this will obviously vary according to age) that such behaviour is not acceptable, for social reasons. Making the child feel guilty about it is not going to smooth her acquisition of the language and making a song-and-dance about swearing only reinforces its effect.

In cases where the parents' own grasp of the language is weak, they might find they need to be extra-careful, or even to appeal for outside help. An English language teacher who had settled with his young family in France recalls: 'Within a few weeks of our arrival here, the two children had picked up an enormous amount of French at school, whilst we still had a lot of trouble making ourselves understood. There was another child in the same age group living in the same block of flats as us and they started playing together in the yard outside. A few days later, this child's mother appeared at our front door, very tight-lipped. We had charming children, she was delighted her child had found two little friends, and so on – *but* "there are words, Monsieur . . ." and she fluttered her hands and rolled her eyes expressively. We found ourselves in the awful position of having to ask her what these words were. "*Gros mots*" ("swear-words"), she replied. "Yes, but (this with much clearing of throats) what *are* the *gros mots* of your otherwise so beautiful a language?" By now, faces were scarlet on both sides. But then, taking her courage in both hands, the lady stepped inside our front door, which she closed carefully behind her, and told us.'

Should your efforts fail to tame the child's swearing, you might try introducing a surrogate, or what Robert Graves called a 'non-alcoholic swear-word'. 'Emily had picked up this really foul swear-word (I can't imagine where) and we were due to visit her grandparents. She was only four, and no amount of friendly persuasion could stop her using it every few minutes – usually at the top of her voice. So one day I let her hear me say, in a moment of great stress: "Oh, moccasins!". She was onto it like lightning. "Moccasins, moccasins, moccasins!" I reacted in a very heavy-handed way. "Emily, how could you, where on earth did you learn such a word, what would Grandma say?" etc., etc. It worked like magic. She spent the next few weeks muttering "moccasins!" every time anything displeased her even slightly – and the visit to her grandparents passed off without incident.'

Finally, and without wishing to seem to recommend the habit, it has to be admitted that the ability to swear *convincingly* in a language is a mark of solidarity with and acceptance by the other speakers of that language. No one who is perceived as a foreigner, no matter how perfectly she speaks the language, can ever get away with it. As someone remarked on a similar occasion: 'The words are there, but the music is lacking'.

Television

With television transmitted by satellite, channels in very many languages have become available almost anywhere in the world to people able to obtain the right equipment. So it is interesting to ask what the role of television is in a child's acquisition of his two languages.

This question has two associated aspects: the development of a child's *linguistic* skill on the one hand, and heightening his *cultural* awareness on the other. As regards the former, television can clearly be a source of rich linguistic input, but only insofar as the child is interested in and motivated by the programmes in question. Moreover, the limitations of a medium of one-way communication also need to be overcome, though this can be done very easily by making watching TV a group activity involving other members of the family or neighbours' children, so that questions can be asked and the programmes discussed together afterwards.

A difficulty arises from the fact that the very programmes that seem likely to satisfy a child's linguistic needs are the ones he is likely to find uninteresting. What he needs is exposure to the widest possible range of accents, voices, genres and functions of language, and television is indeed ideally equipped to do this job, as a glance at a typical afternoon's viewing will show: a do-it-yourself programme, news and weather forecast, gardener's question time, a pop show and a documentary on wildlife show what a rich medium this can be. However, children's TV (with a few exceptions) does not always display this variety, so that for the linguistic kicks all children yearn for they often have to turn to cartoons and commercials.

With these reservations in mind, though, it is fair to say that television provides an excellent tool for training in comprehension. The inherent richness of the medium, its convenience and availability, and the presence of both sound and image all combine to make it an excellent source of raw material for a child to work on.

Where neither of the parents speaks the 'television language', and where the child is therefore in a 'foreign home', the role of television as a source of cultural information can also be very important: this is how French people sit at table, this is what English people eat for breakfast, now is the time of day when the Dutch have their evening meal. But television can play a further, equally important role as it provides children with viewing experiences that they share with others of the same age who speak their weaker language. Whether one likes it or not, the existence of a 'global culture' means that throughout much of the world one is likely to find identical television programmes ('The Simpsons', 'Sesame Street', 'Friends', and so on), familiarity with which will be useful on visits to other countries.

However, 'international' programmes of this kind can also be a source of extreme irritation to bilinguals, and a number of the children in our study felt strongly enough about this to comment on it. The problem is *dubbing*, where a new soundtrack in, say, Spanish replaces the original English or German one. For the bilingual who can often *see* what the original words were, this can be a most disturbing experience, unpleasant enough to make him switch off a programme he had been really looking forward to. So although we have no evidence that watching dubbed programmes has ever done anyone any harm, parents might feel that it is best to avoid them where possible.

For some reason this does not seem to apply to subtitled programmes: not because the bilingual is left free to listen to the original version, but because the majority of children we spoke to thoroughly enjoy comparing the soundtrack with the translation. 'When it's done well, it's a real pleasure, you feel "Ah, that's just right"; when it's not, it's often good for a laugh.' 'I have to put a sheet of paper over the writing to stop myself reading all the time'.

The increasing availability of video recorders has extended the potential of television for bilingual families even further. Many families have informal exchange arrangements. When one recalls how much children (and their parents) talk about what they saw last night on television, and the way in which catch-phrases and commercial slogans penetrate daily conversation, one sees that this is an efficient and enjoyable way of maintaining a second language.

Very young children

Broadly speaking, very small children seem to learn two languages simultaneously as they would learn one: they 'have bilingualism as a mother tongue'. Similarly, successive bilinguals acquire their second language as they acquired their first. In both cases, the phases and stages the children pass through, the order in which the various rules, structures and functions are mastered and the types of 'mistakes' that they make are much the same as for a monolingual child.

There are important implications here for parents. The first is that children below about eight years of age are most unlikely to need any formal teaching or language lessons. We agree completely with the nursery teacher at the United Nations school in Paris, attended by children of 46 nationalities, who is quoted by V. Cook (1979)* as saying:

> The best way to encourage the acquisition of a new language for the child
> is to have happy experiences with friendly persons in sympathetic sur-
> roundings, where learning is spontaneous and done quite unconsciously.

Provided small children are happy and surrounded by a rich linguistic environment in which they have the chance to hear and use their languages in the widest variety of ways, they will learn them. Moreover, they usually do so with an ease and rapidity that seems to their parents (especially if they are themselves struggling with one of the languages in question) little short of miraculous.

Apart from her parents, the bilingual child's most important 'teachers' are other small children, and this is equally true for both languages. Every effort should be made to ensure that regular contacts do take place. The ideal instrument for this is, of course, the playgroup or nursery school. In some countries, such as France, where free nursery education is available to all children between the ages of two and six, this presents no problem at all. In others, parents may find that the only way of getting the child into a playgroup is by organising one themselves. Experience gained in a

---

* We warmly recommend V. Cook's clear and sensible book *Young Children and Language* to readers interested in this topic. Although he concentrates on children learning just one language, what he has to say applies equally to infant and childhood bilinguals precisely because the processes involved seem so similar.

playgroup is extremely valuable to any child: for the child who has just arrived from abroad or who does not speak the community language at home, attendance at such a group will probably be the single most important language-learning opportunity available.

It is usually the case that the child cannot attend playgroups in both her languages, though where this *can* be arranged, however occasionally and informally, it is an excellent thing. This does place an extra responsibility on the parents in question to play and talk with the child even more. It does not mean, though, that the child will find it more difficult to learn the 'second' language (although almost inevitably she will speak it in a more 'adult' way than children usually do). It is perhaps worth recalling here that recent research indicates that, where small children are concerned, progress in one language results in progress in both, although it may take a certain amount of time for this to show.

This is a major point in favour of bilingualism, since it means that parents can encourage the 'home' language or languages confident in the knowledge that, far from being detrimental, this will have a positive effect on their child's learning of the 'second' or outside language. There is no problem here of having to 'rob Peter to pay Paul'. Although we do not fully understand the process, there is evidence of *positive transfer*, that is, when the child acquires a linguistic notion or skill in one language she will find a way of transferring it, when needed, to her second language. This has been confirmed by large-scale studies of immigrant children: those children whose parents have maintained the language of their country of origin in a positive way are more successful with their second language than those whose parents have either dropped their mother tongue or who seriously neglect it. The better the child learns her 'home' language, the better she learns the community language.

There is another important pointer for parents here, which is that talking to children in a language in which you are not fully competent may not be the favour you think it is. Obviously this is a relative matter and only the parents themselves can judge how well they speak the language in question. But it is rather sad and illogical to see a parent – usually the mother – having problems communicating with her child in order to avoid the 'dangers' of bilingualism. In general, we believe that parents do best to teach their children their own language well, rather than another language badly. On the other hand, we have no evidence that a parent's speaking to a child in a 'foreign' language has ever caused permanent problems for the child. However, it seems at best a waste of effort and at worst a serious impoverishment of the parent–child relationship.

Visitors

The presence of visitors at home (by visitors we mean friends and neighbours and their children, relatives, the man who reads the meter, etc.) is natural and welcome. None the less, from the linguistic point of view it can sometimes pose a problem, since it may involve a disruption of the family's habits. Of course, if the visitor happens to be bilingual in the languages in question, then he can be fitted into the existing arrangements. Grandmother Uhr, for example, when she comes to stay with her daughter and son-in-law, speaks Swedish with her daughter and grandchildren, but English with her son-in-law, just as her own daughter does.

In many cases, though, the practical constraints of the situation mean that the language habits will have to be modified in some way. In our experience, most families do adopt simple, effective strategies for dealing with this situation. However, the same family may have different strategies for different visitors which makes their overall behaviour more difficult to describe. Important criteria for choosing a strategy include:

i) Is the visitor a close member of the family (a new in-law, for example)? If this is the case, extra efforts may be made – to teach the newcomer the second language, for example – as a sort of investment.
ii) Is the visitor's stay to be a short one or a long one?
iii) Is the visitor a child or an adult?

The most common strategies we have observed are:

i) All members of the family switching to the visitor's language for the duration of his visit.
ii) Members of the family continuing amongst themselves as before, and using the visitor's language only when addressing him directly.
iii) Members of the family continuing amongst themselves as before when addressing remarks individually to one another but switching to the visitor's language for all general matters and for all remarks directed to him personally.
iv) A member or members of the family providing a simultaneous interpretation for the visitor.

All these strategies have their advantages and disadvantages. If the visitor comes for a really long stay, then (i) may prove something of a strain or even result in a change in the family's system. Strategies (ii) and (iv) work well for short periods, for example, a neighbour's children dashing in for a few minutes, but begin to seem awkward when used for longer periods or with adults. We would guess that (i) and (iii) are the strategies most commonly resorted to and have observed them being used easily and efficiently. None the less, there are occasions when neither is possible – when, for example, monolingual members of both sides of the family are present, which can make strategy (iv) more or less obligatory. Several people mentioned this situation specifically as being very heavy-going.

Visitors will, of course, be tempted to comment on and even wonder at their hosts' 'strange' habits. By and large overt discussion of this kind does no harm to children, provided it is based on at least a minimum of tolerance and commonsense. In our opinion, even a little praise and admiration at the childrens' language abilities is not necessarily a bad thing; a *little* goes a long way though – we are talking about self-confidence, not a swollen head.

Writing

Writing is very often a Cinderella skill as far as bilingual children are concerned, coming well below speaking, understanding and reading in order of priority. Insofar as this is usually a reflection of the child's needs, most parents are content to leave it at that, knowing that the child will learn to write one language properly at school. This means accepting the fact that, for a time at least, there will be a considerable gap between the child's written performances in the two languages. This gap can disappear very quickly, though, if the language is studied at secondary school, for example, or if the situation requires it in some other way.

The main thing is to find occasions for writing and people to write to. Games are the best incentive: one example is 'treasure hunts' where the children hide, for instance, cooking utensils in the house and they have to give you information in writing as to their whereabouts.

The children can also 'write' to the family. They send their works of art to their grandparents, aunts, cousins, etc. when at playgroup, and sign and dedicate them or give them titles and add explanations. These rarely fail to get encouraging replies. From about seven onwards, creating cartoon strips appears to be very successful. One can also use an older child's talent to create stories and to make 'real' books for a younger child. These can then be used for the bedtime reading to the baby of the family.

When a child engages in this kind of activity, it is best not to correct mistakes but rather to make it as enjoyable an activity as possible. From time to time a game of the 'find the error' type can be introduced. It usually goes down very well, particularly if you encourage a child to look things up in the dictionary or in books she has read, in order to play the game.

If the child has no opportunity to go to school in the country where her weaker language is spoken, then it is useful to make up little 'activity books' centred on her life and favourite stories. If it is possible for the child to go to school – even for a very short time – in her weaker language, do not forget to ensure she knows the conventions about the handwritten form of the language. This can be very puzzling and make a child's life difficult unnecessarily. In French, reading *Babar* is probably the best way of making a child accustomed to the script expected from French children in schools. It is also useful to make the children read aloud the letters received from the family and friends. At the pre-reading stage, simply make them guess where the letters come from, with your thumb on the stamp of the envelope!

Quotations

A French / English six-year-old bilingual boy:

> *Bof! C'est normal . . . mais ça doit être embêtant de n'avoir qu'une langue, parce-qu'on doit être coincé quand on voyage.* ('Oh, it's just ordinary . . . but it must be awkward having only one language, because you must get stuck when you travel.')

An English / French fourteen-year-old bilingual girl:

> 'It saves a lot of trouble when you think how hard you have to work to learn a language at school and even then they don't learn it properly.'

An English / French bilingual adult:

> 'I don't think speaking two languages is so extraordinary, but on the other hand, speaking only one language must be a bit odd, like only seeing with one eye: you'd somehow lack the depth or perspective.'

An English / French / Swedish five-year-old trilingual girl:

> 'I like it. You can learn much more songs!'

A French / English fourteen-year-old bilingual boy:

> 'I don't really think about it; it's just a habit. But think if we went back to England and we couldn't speak to various relatives that'd be horrible! The

only thing is at school they keep asking you to do their homework for them
...'

A French / English bilingual adult:

'I can't imagine only speaking one language. I just wouldn't be *me*. People
talk about bilinguals having identity problems. That's rubbish as far as I'm
concerned. If they took away one of my languages, they'd take away half
my identity. And anyway, how do they *manage*?'

A French / German bilingual fifteen-year-old girl:

'I like it. It's nice. It's just fun. And you make more friends more easily.'

Finally, here is what an eminent scholar, himself a Norwegian / English
bilingual, had to say:

I have been bilingual as far back as I can remember, but it was not until I
began reading the literature on the subject that I realised what this meant.
Without knowing it, I had been exposed to untold dangers of retardation,
intellectual impoverishment, schizophrenia, anomie and alienation, most
of which I had apparently escaped, if only by a hair's breadth. If my parents
knew about these dangers, they firmly dismissed them and made me bilingual willy-nilly. They took the position that I would learn all the English I
needed from my playmates and my teachers, and that only by learning and
using Norwegian in the home could I maintain a fruitful contact with them
and their friends and their culture. In the literature I found little mention
of this aspect. What I found was a long parade of intelligence tests proving
bilinguals to be intellectually and scholastically handicapped . . . My own
happy experience with bilingualism, which enabled me to play roles in two
worlds rather than one, was apparently not duplicated by most of those
whom the researchers studied.

(Haugen, 1972)

Recommended resources

Books

Arnberg, L. (1987) *Raising Children Bilingually: The Pre-school Years.* Clevedon:
Multilingual Matters Ltd.
Bialystock, E. (2001) *Bilingualism in Development: Language, Literacy and
Cognition.* Cambridge: Cambridge University Press.
Cook, V. J. (1979) *Young Children and Language.* London: Edward Arnold.

Cunningham-Andersson, U. and Andersson, S. (1999) *Growing Up with two Languages: A Practical Guide.* London, Routledge.

de Jong, E. (1986) *The Bilingual Experience.* Cambridge: Cambridge University Press.

Döpke, S. (1992) *One Parent, One Language: An Interactional Approach.* Amsterdam: John Benjamins.

Dunn, O. (1994) *Help your child with a Foreign Language: A Parents' Handbook.* London: Hodder and Stroughton.

Grosjean, F. (1982) *Life with Two Languages. An Introduction to Bilingualism.* Cambridge, Mass.: Harvard University Press.

Kenner, C. (2000) *Home pages: Literacy Links for Bilingual Children.* Stoke-on-Trent: Trentham Books.

Lyons, J. (1996) *Becoming Bilingual: Language Acquisition in a Bilingual Community.* Clevedon: Multilingual Matters.

Romaine, S. (1995) *Bilingualism.* 2nd ed., Oxford: Blackwell.

Saunders, G. (1988) *Bilingual Children: From Birth to Teens.* Clevedon: Multilingual Matters.

(1982) *Bilingual Children: Guidance for the Family.* Clevedon: Multilingual Matters.

Tokuhama-Espinosa, T. (2001) *Raising Multilingual Children: Foreign Language Acquisition and Children.* Westport, CT: Bergen & Garvey.

Newsletter

The *Bilingual Family Newsletter*, published quarterly by Multilingual Matters Ltd, Cleveland, is designed specifically with parents in mind. It is informative and reliable.

Bibliography

An excellent source of references concerning Minority Languages in Europe is Tjeerdsma, R. S. and Stuijt, M. B. (eds.) (1996) *Bilingualism and Education: A Bibliography on European Regional or Minority Languages.* Ljouwert/Leeuwarden: Fryske Akademy & Mercator-Education.

Journals

Academic Journals that parents might wish to consult on particular topics include:
Bilingualism: Language and Cognition
Language Acquisition: A Journal of Developmental Linguistics
Papers and Reports on Child Language Development
The Bilingual Review / La Revista Bilingüe
International Journal of Bilingual Education and Bilingualism
The International Journal of Bilingualism

Internet sites

There are many sites that provide information, whether about resources such as bilingual books or about services such as immersion courses or bilingual childcare. In order to search for the things you need, simply go to a net browser, type in http://www.yahoo.com, or the address of any other search engine you know, and then type in 'bilingual families' or 'bilingual children' at the search window.

The Bilingual Families Web Page – http://www.nethelp.no/cindy/biling-fam.html – is a useful place to start if you wish to discuss issues with others. There are lots of links to learning resources too.

National Clearing House for Bilingual Education – http://www.ncbe.gwu.edu/ – contains links for bilingual parenting and early language learning which can be very useful to parents all over the world) although this site is primarily relevant to the US context (it is funded by the US Education Department).

References

Aellen, C. and Lambert, W. E. (1969) 'Ethnic identification and personality adjustments of Canadian adolescents of mixed English–French parentage' *Canadian Journal of Behavioural Science* 1, pp. 69–86.

Antier, E. (2001) *Elever mon enfant aujourd'hui.* Paris: Robert Laffont.

Arnberg, L. (1981) 'A longitudinal study of language development in four young children exposed to English and Swedish in the home' *Linköping Studies in Education Reports* 6, Department of Education: Linköping University.

(1987) *Raising Children Bilingually: The Pre-school Years.* Clevedon: Multilingual Matters Ltd.

Arsenian, S. (1937) 'Bilingualism and mental development' *Teachers' College Contribution to Education* 712. New York: Columbia University.

Baetens Beardsmore, H. (1982) *Bilingualism: Basic Principles.* Clevedon: Tieto Ltd.

Baker, C. (2001) *Foundations of Bilingual Education and Bilingualism.* 3rd ed. Clevedon: Multilingual Matters Ltd.

Bere, M. (1924) *A Comparative Study of the Mental Capacity of Children of Foreign Parentage.* New York: Teachers College, Columbia University Press.

Berlin, B. and Kay, P. (1969) *Basic Colour Terms: Their Universality and Evolution.* Berkeley: University of California Press.

Bialystock, E. (2001) *Bilingualism in Development: Language, Literacy and Cognition.* Cambridge: Cambridge University Press.

Bloodstein, O. (1995) *A Handbook on Stuttering.* London: Chapman and Hall.

Bloomfield, L. (1933) *Language.* New York: Holt, Rinehart and Winston.

Brodie, F. W. (1967) *The Devil Drives.* Harmondsworth: Penguin.

Bubenik, V. (1978) 'The acquisition of Czech in the English environment' in M. Paradis (ed.) *Aspects of Bilingualism.* pp. 3–12. Columbia: Hornbeam Press, Inc.

Burling, R. (1959) 'Language development of a Garo- and English-speaking child' *Word* 15, pp. 45–68. Reprinted in E. Hatch (ed.) *Second Language Acquisition. A Book of Readings.* pp. 38–55. Rowley, Mass.: Newbury House.

Byram, M. (1977) *Teaching and Assessing Intercultural Communicative Competence.* Clevedon: Multicultural Matters.

Carrol, C. W. (1978) 'La France devant les questions linguistiques' *Language Problems and Language Planning*, pp. 115–6.

Casse, P. (1984) *Les Outils de la Communication Efficace.* Paris: Chotard.

Celce-Murcia, M. (1975) 'Phonological factors in vocabulary acquisition: A case study of a two-year-old English–French bilingual' *TESOL Conference*, Los Angeles. Reprinted in E. Hatch (ed.) (1978) *Second Language Acquisition. A Book of Readings*, pp. 38–53. Rowley, Mass.: Newbury House.

Cenoz, J. and Genesee, F. (eds.)(2001) *Trends in Bilingual Acquisition.* Amsterdam: John Benjamins.

Clyne, M. G. (1967) *Transference and Triggering.* The Hague: Nijhoff.

Coleman, J. A. (1996) *Studying Languages: A Survey. The Proficiency, Background, Attitudes and Motivations of Students of Foreign Languages in the United Kingdom and Europe.* London: Centre for Information on Language Teaching and Research.

Cook, V. J. (1979) *Young Children and Language.* London: Edward Arnold.

Coulmas, F. (1989) *The Writing Systems of the World.* Oxford: Blackwell.

Council of Europe (2001) *Common European Framework of Reference for Languages: Learning, teaching, assessment.* Cambridge: Cambridge University Press.

(1997) *The Cambridge Encyclopedia of Language.* Cambridge: Cambridge University Press.

Crystal, D. (2000) *Language Death.* Cambridge: Cambridge University Press.

Cunningham-Andersson, U. and Andersson, S. (1999) *Growing Up with two languages: a practical guide.* London: Routledge.

Darcy, N. T. (1953) 'Bilingualism and the measurement of intelligence: Review of a decade of research' *Journal of Genetic Psychology* 103, pp. 259–82.

De Houwer, A. (1999) 'Environmental factors in early bilingual development: The role of parental beliefs and attitudes' in Extra, G. and Verhoeven, L. (eds.) *Bilingualism and Migration.* Berlin: Mouton de Gruyter, pp. 75–95.

de Jong, E. (1986) *The Bilingual Experience.* Cambridge: Cambridge University Press.

DeLoache and Gottlieb (2000) *A World of Babies.* Cambridge: Cambridge University Press.

Deuchar, M. and Quay, S. (2000) *Bilingual Acquisition: Theoretical Implications of a Case Study.* Oxford: Oxford University Press.

Deuchar, M. and Vihman, M. (2002) 'Language contact in early bilinguals: the special status of function words' in Jones, M. and Esch, E. (eds.) *Language Change: The Interplay of Internal, External and Extra-linguistic Factors.* Contributions to the Sociology of Language Series. Berlin: Mouton.

Diller, K. C. (1970) '"Compound" and "coordinate" bilingualism: a conceptual artefact' *Word* 26, pp. 254–61.

Dimitrijević, N. J. (1965) 'A bilingual child' *English Language Teaching* 20, pp. 23–8.

Döpke, S. (1992) *One Parent, One Language: An Interactional Approach.* Amsterdam: John Benjamins.

Doyle, A. B., Champagne, M. and Segalowitz, N. (1978) 'Some issues in the assessment of linguistic consequences of early bilingualism' *Working Papers on Bilingualism* 14, pp. 21–31.

Driscoll, P. and Frost D. (eds.) (1999) *The Teaching of Modern Languages in the Primary School.* London: Routledge.

Duranti, A. (1997) *Linguistic Anthropology.* Cambridge: Cambridge University Press.

Efron, D. (1972) *Gesture, Race and Culture*. The Hague: Mouton.

Elwert, W. T. (1959) *Das Zweisprachige Individuum: Ein Selbstzeugnis*. Mainz: Verlag der Akademie des Wissenschaften und Literatur.

Ervin-Tripp, S. (1961) 'Semantic shift in bilingualism' *American Journal of Psychology* 74, pp. 233–41.

Ervin, S. M. and Osgood, C. E. (1954) 'Second language learning and bilingualism' *Journal of Abnormal and Social Psychology*, Supplement, 49, pp. 139–46.

Fantini, A. E. (1976) *Language Acquisition of a Bilingual Child: A Sociolinguistic Perspective*. Vermont: The Experiment Press.

 (1978) 'Bilingual behavior and social cues: case studies of two bilingual children' in M. Paradis (ed.) *Aspects of Bilingualism*, pp. 283–301. Columbia: Hornbeam Press, Inc.

Ferguson, C. A. (1959) 'Diglossia' *Word* 15, pp. 325–40.

Fillmore, L. W. (1979) 'Individual differences in second language acquisition' in C. J. Fillmore, D. Kempler and W. S-Y. Wang (eds.) *Individual Differences in Language Ability and Language Behavior*, pp. 203–28. New York: Academic Press.

Fishman, J. (1989) *Language and Ethnicity in Minority Sociolinguistic Perspective*. Clevedon: Multilingual Matters.

Fishman, J. (1991) *Reversing Language Shift*. Clevedon: Multilingual Matters.

Foley, W. (1997) *Anthropological Linguistics*. Oxford: Blackwell.

Gordon, D. C. (1978) 'The French language and national identity (1930–1975)' *Contributions to the Sociology of Language* 22.

Grégoire, Abbé (1999) *Textes Choisis*, preface by Dominique Audrerie. Paris: Editions Confluences.

Grosjean, F. (1982) *Life with Two Languages. An Introduction to Bilingualism*, Cambridge, Mass.: Harvard University Press.

 (1984) 'Le bilinguisme: vivre avec deux langues' *B.U.L.A.G.* 11, pp. 4–25. Besançon: Université de Franche-Comté.

 (1992) 'Another view of bilingualism' in Harris, R. J. (ed.) *Cognitive Processing in Bilinguals*. Amsterdam: North-Holland, pp. 51–62.

Gumperz, J. J. (1982) 'Social network and language shift' in J. J. Gumperz (ed.) *Discourse Strategies*. Cambridge: Cambridge University Press.

Gumperz, J. J. and Levinson, S. C. (1996) *Rethinking Linguistic Relativity*. Cambridge: Cambridge University Press.

Hamers, J. F. and Blanc, M. (1984) *Bilingualité et Bilinguisme*. Bruxelles: P. Mardagua ed.

Harris, B. and Sherwood, B. (1978) 'Translating as an innate skill' in D. Gerver and H. W. Sinaiko (eds.) *Language Interpretation and Communication*. London and New York: Plenum Press.

Hatch, E. (ed.) (1978) *Second Language Acquisition. A Book of Readings*. Rowley, Mass.: Newbury House.

Haugen, E. (1953) *The Norwegian Language in America: A Study of Bilingual Behavior*. (2nd revised edn 1969) Bloomington: Indiana University Press.

(1956) *Bilingualism in the Americas: A Bibliography and Research Guide.* University of Alabama Press.

(1972) 'Bilingualism as a social and personal problem' in R. Filipovic (ed.) *Active Methods and Modern Aids in the Teaching of Foreign Languages,* pp. 1–14. London: OUP.

Herman, J. (1996) '"Grenouille, where are you?" Crosslinguistic transfer in bilingual kindergartners learning to read'. Ph.D. dissertation, Harvard University.

Hoffmann, C. (1991) *An Introduction to Bilingualism,* London: Longman.

Hornberger, N. H. (1990) 'Creating successful learning contexts for bilingual literacy' *Teachers College Record,* 92 (2) 212–229.

Hornby, P. A. (1977) *Bilingualism: Psychological, Social and Educational Implications.* New York: Academic Press, Inc.

Hudson, R. A. (1980) *Sociolinguistics.* Cambridge: Cambridge University Press.

(1981) 'Some issues on which linguists can agree' *Journal of Linguistics* 17, pp. 333–43.

Jones, M. and Esch, E. (eds.) (2002) *Language Change: The Interplay of Internal, External and Extra-linguistic Factors.* Contributions to the Sociology of Language Series. Berlin: Mouton.

Jorgensen, J. N. and Holden, A. (eds.) (1997) *The Development of Successive Bilingualism in School-Age Children,* Copenhagen Studies in Bilingualism 27. Copenhagen: Royal Danish School of Educational Studies.

Keller-Cohen, D. (1979) 'Systematicity and variation in the non-native child's acquisition of conversational skills' *Language Learning* 29 (1), pp. 27–44.

Kramsch, C. (1998) 'The privilege of the intercultural speaker' in Byram, M. and Fleming, M. F. (eds.) *Language Learning in Intercultural Perspective.* Cambridge: Cambridge University Press.

Lam, A. (2001) 'Bilingualism' in Carter, R. and Nunan, D. (eds.) *The Cambridge Guide to Teaching English to Speakers of Other Languages.* Cambridge: Cambridge University Press, pp. 93–99.

Lambert, W. E. and Tucker, G. R. (1972) *Bilingual Education of Children: The St Lambert Experiment.* Rowley, Mass.: Newbury House.

Leopold, W. (1954) 'A child's learning of two languages' *Georgetown University Round Table on Languages and Linguistics* 1954, 7, pp. 19–30. Reprinted in E. Hatch (ed.) *Second Language Acquisition. A Book of Readings,* pp. 23–32. Rowley, Mass.: Newbury House.

Lewis, G. (1981) *Bilingualism and Bilingual Education.* Oxford: Pergamon.

Mackey, W. F. (1962) 'The description of bilingualism' *Canadian Journal of Linguistics* 7, 51–8.

(1967) *Bilingualism as a World Problem.* Montreal: Harvest House.

(1976) *Bilinguisme et Contact des Langues.* Paris: Klinsieck.

Macnamara, J. (1970) 'Bilingualism and thought' in J. Alatis (ed.) *Bilingualism and Language Contact.* Washington, DC: Georgetown University Press.

Macnamara, J. and Kushnir, S. (1971) 'Linguistic independence of bilinguals: the input switch' *Journal of Verbal Learning and Verbal Behavior* 10, pp. 480–7.

McLaughlin, B. (1978) *Second Language Acquisition in Childhood*. Hillsdale, NJ: Lawrence Erlbaum.

Mikeš, M. (1967) 'Acquisition des catégories grammaticales dans le langage de l'enfant' *Enfance* 20, pp. 289–98.

Milroy, L. and Muysken, P. (eds.) (1995) *One Speaker, Two Languages: Cross-disciplinary Perspectives on Code-Switching*. Cambridge: Cambridge University Press.

Nettle, D. and Romaine, S. (2000) *Vanishing Voices: the Extinction of the World's Languages*. Oxford: Oxford University Press.

Oka, H. (1989) 'Bringing up children bilingually in Japan' *Studies in English Language and Literature* 39, 113–133.

Oksaar, E. (1970) 'Zum Spacherwerb des Kindes in Zweisprachiger Umgebung' *Folia Linguistica* 4, pp. 330–58.

(1971) 'Code-switching as an interactional strategy for developing bilingual competence' *Word* 27, pp. 377–85.

(1977) 'On becoming trilingual. A case study' in C. Maloney (ed.) *Deutsch im Kontakt mit anderen Sprachen*, pp. 296–306. Kronberg; Scriptor Verlag.

Paradis, M. (ed.) (1978) *Aspects of Bilingualism*. Columbia: Hornbeam Press, Inc.

Paradis, J. and Genesee, F. (1996) 'Syntactic acquisition in bilingual children: autonomous or interdependent?' *SSLA*, 18, 1–25.

Park, R. E. (1931) 'Personality and cultural conflict' *Publication of the American Sociological Society* 25, pp. 95–110. (Republished in R. E. Park (1964) *Race and Culture*. Glencoe, Illinois: The Free Press.)

Past, A. (1976) *Preschool Reading in Two Languages as a Factor of Bilingualism*. Ph.D. thesis, University of Texas at Austin.

Paulston, C. B. (1975) 'Ethnic relations and bilingual education: accounting for contradictory data' *Working Papers on Bilingualism* 6, pp. 368–401.

Peal, E. and Lambert, W. E. (1962) 'Relation of bilingualism to intelligence' *Psychological Monographs* 76, pp. 1–23.

Perregaux, P. L. (1994) *Les enfants à deux voix: Des effets du bilinguisme sur l'apprentissage de la lecture*. Bern: Peter Lang.

Pfaff, C. W. (1979) 'Constraints on language mixing: intrasentential code-switching and borrowing in Spanish / English' *Language* 55, pp. 291–318.

Poplack, S. (1980) 'Sometimes I'll start a sentence in English y termino en espanol: Toward a typology of code-switching' *Linguistics* 18, pp. 582–618.

Raffler-Engel, W. von (1965) 'Del bilinguismo infantile' *Archivio Glottologica Italiano* 50, pp. 175–80.

Roberts, C., Byram, M., Barro, A., Jordan, S. and Street, B. (2001) *Language Learners as Ethnographers*. Clevedon: Multilingual Matters.

Romaine, S. (1995) *Bilingualism*. 2nd ed., Oxford: Blackwell.

(1999) 'Early bilingual development: from elite to folk' in Extra, G. and Verhoeven, L. (eds.) *Bilingualism and Migration*. Berlin: Mouton de Gruyter, pp. 61–73.

Ronjat, J. (1913) *Le Développement du Langage Observé Chez un Enfant Bilingue.* Paris: Libraire Ancienne H. Champion.

Ruke-Dravina, V. (1967) *Mehrsprachigkeit im Vorschulalter.* Lund: Glesrup.

Saer, O. J. (1923) 'The effects of bilingualism on intelligence' *British Journal of Psychology* 14, pp. 25–38.

Saunders, G. (1982) *Bilingual Children: Guidance for the Family.* Clevedon: Multilingual Matters Ltd.

Scovel, T. (1988) *A Time to Speak: A Psycholinguistic Inquiry into the Critical Period for Human Speech.* Boston, MA: Heinle and Heinle/Newbury House.

Singleton, D. (1989) *Language Acquisition: The Age Factor.* Clevedon: Multilingual Matters.

Smith, M. E. (1935) 'A study of the speech of eight bilingual children of the same family' *Child Development* 6, pp. 19–25.

Snow, C. E. (1977) 'The development of conversation between mothers and babies' *Journal of Child Language* 4.

Snow, C. E. et al. (1991) 'Giving formal definitions: a linguistic or metalinguistic skill?' in Bialystock, E. (ed.) *Language Processing in Bilingual Children.* Cambridge: Cambridge University Press, pp.90–112.

Snow, C. W. and Ferguson, C. A. (eds.) (1977) *Talking to Children: Language Input and Acquisition.* Cambridge: Cambridge University Press.

Srivastava, R. N. (1988) 'Societal bilingualism and bilingual education: A study of the Indian situation' in Paulston, C. B. (ed.) *International Handbook of Bilingualism and Bilingual Education.* New York: Greenwood Press, pp. 247–274.

Taeschner, T. (1983) *The Sun is Feminine. A Study on Language Acquisition in Bilingual Children.* Berlin and Heidelberg: Springer-Verlag.

Tjeerdsma, R. S. and Stuijt, M. B. (eds.) (1996) *Bilingualism and Education: A Bibliography on European Regional or Minority Languages.* Ljouwert/ Leeuwarden: Fryske Akademy & Mercator-Education.

Tokuhama-Espinosa, T. (2001) *Raising Multilingual Children: Foreign Language Acquisition and Children.* Westport, CT: Bergen & Garvey.

Tosi, A. (1982) 'Mother-tongue teaching for the children of migrants' in V. Kinsella (ed.) *Surveys 1, Cambridge Language Teaching Surveys.* Cambridge: Cambridge University Press.

Turner, B. S. (1999) 'The Sociology and Anthropology of the Family' in *Classical Sociology.* London: Sage, Chapter 13.

Ulrike-Kellett, A. and Alarcon-Neve L. J. (2001) 'Language reactivation in bilinguals: evidence of first and second language recovery in bilingual children', Poster, Third International Symposium on Bilingualism, Bristol.

Valdman, A. (1976) *Introduction to French Phonology and Morphology.* Rowley, Mass.: Newbury House.

Van Borsel, J., E. Maes and S. Foulon (2001) 'Stuttering and Bilingualism: A review' *Journal of Fluency Disorders,* 26, 179–205.

Van Overbeke, M. (1972) *Introduction au Bilinguisme*. Bruxelles: Nathan.

Vihman, M. (1999) 'The transition to grammar in a bilingual child: positional patterns, modal learning and relational words', *International Journal of Bilingualism* 3, 267–301.

Volterra, V. and Taeschner, T. (1978) 'The acquisition and development of language by bilingual children' *Journal of Child Language* 5, pp. 311–26.

Watson, I. (2002) 'Convergence in the Brain: how bilinguals' sound systems are and aren't independent', in Jones, M. and Esch, E. (eds.) *Language Change: The Interplay of Internal, External and Extra-linguistic Factors*. Contributions to the Sociology of Language Series. Berlin: Mouton.

Watson, J. B. and Kayser, H. (1994) 'Assessment of bilingual/bicultural children and adults who stutter', *Seminars in Speech and Language*, 15, 149–164.

Weinreich, U. (1953) *Languages in Contact*. The Hague: Mouton.

Wells, G. (1981) *Learning through Interaction: The Study of Language Development*. Cambridge: Cambridge University Press.

Yamamoto, M. (2001) *Language Use in Interlingual Families: A Japanese-English Sociolinguistic Study*. Clevedon: Multilingual Matters.

Zentella, A. C. (1997) *Growing Up Bilingual: Puerto Rican Children in New York*. Malden, MA: Blackwell Publishers.

Zierer, E. (1977) 'Experiences in the bilingual education of a child of preschool age' *International Review of Applied Linguistics* 15, pp. 144–9.

Index